Women in transition

A study of the experiences of Bangladeshi women living in Tower Hamlets

Chris Phillipson, Nilufar Ahmed and Joanna Latimer

The POLICY
P~P
PRESS

First published in Great Britain in April 2003 by

The Policy Press
University of Bristol
Fourth Floor, Beacon House
Queen's Road
Bristol BS8 1QU
UK

Tel no +44 (0)117 331 4054
Fax no +44 (0)117 331 4093
E-mail tpp-info@bristol.ac.uk
www.policypress.org.uk

ISBN 1 86134 510 0

Reprinted 2004

British Library Cataloguing in Publication Data
A catalogue record for this book is available from the British Library

Library of Congress Cataloging-in-Publication Data
A catalog record for this book has been requested

Chris Phillipson is Professor of Applied Social Studies and Social Gerontology in the School of Social Relations at Keele University, **Nilufar Ahmed** is Research Fellow in the School of Social Relations at Keele University and **Joanna Latimer** is a Lecturer in the School of Social Sciences, Cardiff University.

Cover design by Qube Design Associates, Bristol
Printed in Great Britain by Hobbs the Printers Ltd, Southampton

Contents

Acknowledgements

Community-based studies invariably rely upon a large group of people and organisations to make them possible and this one is no exception to this general rule. Many individuals and groups have given generously of their time in helping the research and for this we are enormously grateful. We would like to give particular thanks to Fauzia Ahmad, John Eversley, Mibi Ismail, Roseanna Pollen and Saheed Ullah. They provided a range of advice, access to local resources, and a sounding board for ideas. The research would not have been possible without their support and enthusiasm. We are also grateful to Kate Gavron, from the Institute of Community Studies, who provided helpful suggestions based on her own research in the area.

A range of organisations in Tower Hamlets provided assistance to the study. We would like to mention in particular: Tower Hamlets Parents Centre, APASENTH, The Graduates' Forum, Jagonari, Mulberry Girls' School, St.Dunstans, Dame Colet House, and Social Action for Health. We are also grateful for the assistance given by the following: Albion Health Centre, Bethnal Green Health Centre, Chrisp St. Health Centre, Jubilee St. Health Centre, St. Stephens Health Centre, and Wapping Health Centre. The Nania Research Centre provided excellent assistance with interviews, transcribing tapes and with photographs of the area. We are very grateful indeed for their support.

Graham Allan and Amanda Grenier provided valuable comments on drafts of the report. Jennifer Swindle gave research support and advice at a crucial stage of the work and we are greatly in her debt. Sue Humphries did an excellent job on the production of successive drafts of the report. We are especially grateful to the Nuffield Foundation which provided financial support to the project. Sharon Witherspoon, Deputy Director of the Foundation, was consistently supportive of the project throughout the various phases of the research. Finally, we must thank in particular all the women who agreed to be interviewed for the study. They had some remarkable stories to tell and we hope we have managed to convey some of the issues and concerns affecting their lives.

Chris Phillipson (Keele University)
Nilufar Ahmed (Keele Unversity)
Joanna Latimer (Cardiff University)

Introduction to the study

This study focuses on the lives of 100 women, living in the London Borough of Tower Hamlets, who migrated to the UK during the 1970s through to the early 1990s from the Sylhet district of Bangladesh. The report examines the family and community life of these women and considers the changes introduced by what has been termed 'transnational migration' (Ballard, 1994; Phizacklea, 1999; Levitt, 2001). The origin of this work stems from research on older people living in the Bethnal Green district of Tower Hamlets (Phillipson et al, 2001). This research included a small number of older people, originally from Bangladesh, who were found to be living in conditions of considerable hardship. These households also included female spouses, usually much younger than their husbands, together with a large number of dependent children. The findings from the research stimulated an interest in investigating further the social and economic circumstances of this group of women. A review of the literature revealed only a limited number of studies of Bangladeshi women, with particular neglect of those in their middle years. Such women are, however, likely to play a crucial role in respect of informal care, often providing support to younger as well as older people living in the same household. Caring itself is likely to take place in conditions of intense deprivation (judged on the basis of national surveys comparing Bangladeshis with other groups), often creating problems of isolation and social exclusion (Kabeer, 2000).

Given these observations, and given the work already available on younger and older Bangladeshis, it was proposed to undertake a study of women in the middle generation (aged 35-55). The reasoning behind selecting this group was as follows:

- Little is known about the full range of roles and responsibilities of this group within the extended family.
- There is limited knowledge about how roles may be changing for Bangladeshi women, especially for middle and younger generations.
- Women may experience caring in isolation from sources of help outside the Bangladeshi community (only 4% of Bangladeshi women aged 45 and over are able to speak English fluently or fairly well) (HEA, 2000).
- The migration histories and experiences of Bangladeshi women have so far gone unrecorded in the research literature.
- There are important policy issues to be considered in delivering effective support to the Bangladeshi community, and to women in particular.

This study explores and analyses these questions in three main ways. First, through interviews with 100 first generation Bangladeshi women living in the London Borough of Tower Hamlets; second, through group interviews with women in their late teens and early twenties; third, through interviews with leaders of relevant organisations within the Tower Hamlets community. The report on the results of the research is divided into five main sections. First, existing literature on the Bangladeshi community is reviewed, with a focus on findings from national surveys as well as locality-based research. Second, this material is related to theoretical debates about the nature of transnational migration, particularly in relation to discussions concerning gender and identity. Third, the methodology behind the study is discussed, and the key research questions summarised. Fourth, the main findings are presented, beginning with recollections from the women about the experience of migration and concluding with reflections about expectations for the future. Finally, there is a discussion about the policy implications of the study. We begin, however, with a review of existing research on Bangladeshis in Britain, identifying some of the key findings of relevance for our own work.

History and background

The Bangladeshi population in Britain is a significant group within the ethnic minority population, and was identified as the "youngest and fastest growing of all the ethnic populations recorded in the 1991 Census of Great Britain" (Eade et al, 1996, p 150). Although the distinctiveness of the Bangladeshi community, as compared with other South Asian groups, has been acknowledged, variations according to region, age cohort, social class and gender have been given rather less attention. However, differences are likely to increase over time, especially in respect of variations between women and men, and between age groups (Gardner and Shukur, 1994; Gardner, 2002).

Bangladeshis in Britain originate mainly from the Sylhet district in north-east Bangladesh, which after the Punjab and Gujarat has been the third largest source of immigration from South Asia (Ballard, 1994b). Sylhet, although more prosperous than other parts of Bangladesh, is significantly poorer in comparison to the other two areas – a fact that has had long-term implications for patterns of adjustment by migrants in the UK (Ballard, 1994b; Gardner, 1995). First generation migrants spoke a variety of dialects and there was a low standard of literacy in standard Bengali (Kershen, 2000). In respect to religion, Sunni Muslims formed the majority. Most migrants came from a network of rural villages within the region and in respect of social origins were drawn mainly from peasant farming families. Gardner and Shukur comment that:

> Such owner-occupiers formed a distinct rural class, and when the opportunities for overseas migration appeared they were in a better position to raise the capital outlay for their fares, if necessary by mortgaging their land. In sharp contrast to landless families where every pair of hands was vital for day-to-day production either through subsistence

agriculture or wage-earning, landowning households could often spare the labour of one or even two of its young men. Their greater financial independence also meant that they were more accustomed to thinking of long-term investment, enterprise and profit than their landless neighbours. (1994, p 146)

The earliest arrivals from Sylhet (who can be traced back at least to the 19th century) were invariably seamen or *lascars* employed on Britain's mercantile fleet. Some stayed in Britain on a temporary basis waiting to secure a return passage – usually on a ship bound for India. However, others stayed for longer periods, in some cases, as Eade notes (1997a), living with or marrying local white women and establishing a home (usually in areas close to the ports from which they had embarked). Eade summarises this process:

> ... [the] two world wars stimulated the employment of Sylheti and other workers from the Bengal delta in Britain's mercantile fleet. The increased presence of Bengali and other migrant workers ... in London, Cardiff, Liverpool, South Shields and other ports was the focus of local hostility in the years following the end of the First World War. The first oral accounts from Bengali *lascars* who came here before and during the Second World War suggest an increase not only of those employed on British ships but also in the number of sailors who 'jumped ship' and found work in cities across the country. Some of these sailors stayed for long periods of their adult lives in urban neighbourhoods where they found the rudiments for a distinctive community life through lodging houses, cafes, restaurants and other small businesses as well as the establishment of religious facilities. (1997a, p 92)

By the 1940s, larger numbers of Bangladeshis were beginning to search for employment in factories and restaurants in various parts of England. Choudhury (1993) records around 400 Bangladeshis from Sylhet living in London (mainly the East End) during the 1940s. He notes that these early job seekers (predominantly male) often found it hard to secure employment, with many moving to the Midlands and the North of England to work in the manufacturing and textiles industries. Eade (1999) suggests that by the 1960s there were approximately 6,000 Bangladeshi men scattered across different urban centres in England. Gardner sets the scene:

Arriving as young men in the postwar period, most lived and worked in northern cities such as Birmingham and Oldham, finding employment in heavy industry. Some went directly to London, working in the garment trade as pressers or tailors. Usually living in lodging houses with other Sylhetis, this was a period of unremittingly hard work, a major factor shaping the men's identities. As much money was saved each month as possible, and sent back to Sylhet. According to conventional accounts of this period, the men were 'sojourners' rather than 'settlers'. (1998, p 163)

Gardner (1997, p 163) notes that with the recession of the 1970s and 1980s this process went into reverse, with many Sylheti men returning to London to seek work in the garment or restaurant trades. They were to be joined in this period by an increasing number of wives and dependants as well as female partners from new marriages in Bangladesh. By the time of the 1991 Census, 53% of the total Bangladeshi population in Britain could be found in the Greater London area, with a quarter of British Bangladeshis located in the London Borough of Tower Hamlets.

Research findings on Bangladeshis in Britain

Research on (or including) the Bangladeshi community has come from a variety of sources, including: Census data (Eade et al, 1996); the Fourth National Survey of Ethnic Minorities (NSEM) (Modood et al, 1997); the Health Survey for England (Erens et al, 2001); analysis of large data sets such as the Labour Force Survey (LFS) and General Household Survey (GHS) (Evandrou, 2000; Dale et al, 2001a, 2001b; Zorlu, 2001); locality-based ethnographic research (Khanum, 1994; Eade, 1997a, 1997b; Gardner, 1997, 1998, 2002; Qureshi, 1998; Phillipson et al, 2000, 2001); research on health and social care issues (Dutt, 1995; Nazroo, 1997; Silveira and Ebrahim, 1998); and comparative research with samples from Bangladesh as well as Britain (Kabeer, 2000; Burholt et al, 2002).

The 1991 Census confirmed that the Bangladeshi population in Britain had a number of characteristics distinguishing it from other South Asian groups. According to Eade et al:

This distinctiveness relates to the rapid and continuing growth of the Bangladeshi population, the very high proportion of young people, the large family size, the concentration of residents within Greater London, and especially Tower Hamlets, the high degree of segregation, the low socio-economic status and the dependence on local authority housing. (1996, p 151)

The 1991 Census recorded 163,000 Bangladeshis, with just under half below the age of 16, and around three quarters under 35. By the time of the 2001 Census the population had increased by 97,000 to 260,000. The National Survey of Ethnic Minorities (NSEM) carried out in 1994, found 48% of Bangladeshi respondents to be under the age of 15, 48% aged 16-59, and 4% over 60 (Modood et al, 1997). A feature of the population to the 1980s was an excess of males with 1991 Census data showing 10% more males than females. One reason for this is the different migration history of Bangladeshis when compared with other South Asian groups, with the characteristic pattern of men migrating first and subsequently being joined in Britain (often at a much later date) by their wives. This is a feature of South Asian migration, but is particularly noticeable among Bangladeshis who were the last to complete the migration of whole families (Ballard, 1994b). In line with this, the NSEM found that three out of ten Bangladeshi adults (mostly women and adult children) had arrived in Britain since the mid-1980s.

Bangladeshis are also distinctive in respect of household size, with 60% of households comprising five or more people, as compared with less than 8% of total households of this size (Eade et al, 1996). Large families are thus relatively commonplace in the Bangladeshi community, with more than half of Bangladeshi women in their late thirties having four or more children. The NSEM found that 88% of Bangladeshi couples had children in comparison with 49% of white couples. Overall, 42% of Bangladeshi families had four or more children (9% have six or more), compared with 4% of white families. On the other hand, Berthoud (2000, p 19) notes that the very high levels of fertility may have been reducing in recent decades, and he estimates that the annual rate of teenage motherhood among Bangladeshi women fell from 61 per thousand in the mid-1980s to 38 per thousand by the mid-1990s. One reason for the reduction of teenage motherhood is likely to

Villagers grouped together for a picture:
– a memento for a migrant (early 1960s)

Group picture of friends before one of them migrated to the UK (1962)

A migrant and his bride on their wedding day in Bangladesh (1970)

Wedding preparations being made in Bangladesh (1960s)

be the later age of marriage for British-born Bangladeshi women, given that having children outside of marriage remains comparatively rare.

Another important feature of the Bangladeshi community concerns its geographical clustering: around 47% of all Bangladeshis in the UK reside in inner London, with Tower Hamlets having the largest proportion. By 2001, 33.4% of the Tower Hamlets population and a majority (over 55%) of school pupils were classified as Bangladeshi. Eade comments that:

> In Tower Hamlets and elsewhere these settlers from the Bengal delta shared a highly segregated existence – the product of the 'combination of recent arrival, young age structure, large and extended families and poor economic situation'. To this list should be added the strong social and cultural ties created through chain migration from the Sylhet countryside. (1997a, p 94)

Research has confirmed the poor living conditions and chronic overcrowding affecting Bangladeshi families. Eade et al (1996) report that, according to Census data, nearly one fifth (19%) of Bangladeshi households live at the highest tabulated density category (over 1.5 persons per room), compared with less than 0.5% of the total resident population and 8% of Pakistani households. Thirty-five per cent of Bangladeshis are council tenants, and 37% live in flats or bedsits. Bangladeshis are also more likely to live in accommodation more than three storeys high: nearly six out of ten did so according to the 1994-95 Survey of English Housing, and a fifth of Bangladeshi flat dwellers live above the third floor. It is also relevant to note (given the size of households) that one in three families lack access to a private garden, yard or patio.

A further measure of overcrowding is the so-called bedroom standard, which sets a standard for the number of bedrooms required by a household depending on its composition and the relation of its members to each other. The standard is then compared with the actual number of bedrooms available to the household. Where the number of rooms is one or more below the bedroom standard, households are classified as overcrowded. Data for 1994-95 indicate that nearly half of Bangladeshi households are below the bedroom standard

compared with only 2% of white households. Given this background, it is probably not surprising that the survey of English housing carried out in 1994-95 found that 40% of Bangladeshi people were slightly or very dissatisfied with their accommodation. The figure for white households was just 7%.

Berthoud (2000) demonstrates the extent to which very high rates of poverty are characteristic of Bangladeshi households. The combined figure for Bangladeshi and Pakistani families, based on data from the NSEM, was an extraordinary 50% of working households living below the poverty line (compared with 9% for white households), and 72% for non-working and non-pensioner households (the figure for white households was 43%). Low wages, high unemployment and household characteristics such as family size, are important causal factors. Zorlu's (2001) analysis of four waves of the British Quarterly Labour Force Survey shows the mean net weekly pay of Pakistanis and Bangladeshis combined as £154.28 (compared with £206.60 for white people). Importantly, barely a quarter (26%) of this group are in medium/high-skilled occupations, in comparison with nearly one in two (48%) of white people. Unemployment and economic inactivity rates remain high for certain age cohorts of Bangladeshis, and for women in particular (LFS data for 1998/99 cited by Dale et al, 2001b, show economic activity rates of 20% for Bangladeshi women aged 16-59, compared with 74% for white women).

Economic and social deprivation is also reflected in the health status of Bangladeshis, with high rates of limiting long-standing illness (LLSI) and self-reported morbidity. The *Health Survey for England 1999* found 72% of Bangladeshi men more likely to report an LLSI in comparison with white men; and 39% of Bangladeshi women more likely as compared with white women (cited in Evandrou, 2000, p 22). Cultural factors also play a role in influencing particular health outcomes (Dutt, 1995). For example, the second Health Education Authority survey of health and lifestyles (HEA, 2000) found that among women aged 50-74, 92% reported that they had chewed tobacco recently, either on its own or with paan or betel nut. An increased risk of mouth and throat cancers has been associated with this activity (Bedi, cited in Evandrou, 2000). Women's position within the family group may also be an important factor in determining access to health care. Khanum's anthropological study of Bangladeshi women in a Manchester community noted that the image of women as self-depriving and submissive encouraged them to "endure physical as well as psychological stress and to depend upon the household head's decision regarding her treatment facilities" (Khanum, 1994, p 289).

Although the overall context presents a picture of deprivation and hardship, variations by region, social class, age cohort and gender are of major importance. Younger cohorts present a more optimistic picture as compared with older cohorts, especially in areas such as educational attainment and employment. Dale et al (2001a), for example, note the significant increase in degree-level education, with an increase of 83% in applications to university from Bangladeshi women over the period 1994-99. This is also likely to translate into higher rates of economic activity, especially in relation to part-time working. In Tower Hamlets, where one quarter of British Bangladeshis reside, there have been significant improvements in the performance of Bangladeshi boys and girls within the school system. For example, the proportion of girls gaining five or more GCSE A-C grades increased from 36.6% in 1998 to 44.2% in 2000 (comparable figures for British white girls were 24.9% and 30%); the figures for boys (white boys in brackets) were: 29.7% (17.6%) and 32.7% (18.1%) (LBTH, no date).

On the other hand, some groups of Bangladeshis will continue to experience disproportionate social and economic problems. Poverty in old age is likely to be a major issue given the limited access of Bangladeshi women and men to private pensions. Ginn and Arber (2001), analysing data from the 1994-96 Family Resources Surveys, found that among those aged 20-59 only 9% of men have either an occupational pension, a personal pension, or a self-employed pension (the figure for white men was 61%); the comparable figure for women (white women in brackets) was 3% (37%). Non-UK born Bangladeshis, who are unlikely to speak fluent English, are especially disadvantaged within the labour market. Dale et al (2001b) (taking Bangladeshi and Pakistani women together) calculate that for those with no qualifications, who are not UK born, do not speak fluent English and have a youngest child under five, the predicted probability of

economic activity is just 1%. The level of activity rises to 24% for women who are UK born and with fluent English, but have no qualifications and a youngest child under five. They conclude:

> We may therefore expect a considerable rise in the economic activity of ... Bangladeshi women simply as a result of the increasing numbers born in the UK and also speaking English. If such women have a higher qualification, the predicted probability of their economic activity rises dramatically. (2001, p 34)

Transnational migration

A major focus of this study is the way in which a group of women have experienced what has been termed 'transnational migration' (Faist, 2000). Following Peggy Levitt, the concern is with "... how ordinary people are incorporated into the countries that receive them while remaining active in the places they come from" (2001, p 4). This relationship has been defined as:

> ... 'transnationalism' [is] the process by which immigrants forge and sustain multi-stranded social relations that link together their societies of origin and settlement. We call these processes transnationalism to emphasize that many immigrants today build social fields that cross geographic, cultural and political borders.... An essential element is the multiplicity of involvements that transmigrants sustain both in home and host societies. (Basch et al, 1994, p 6)

Some of the questions that arise include: what kind of social networks are generated and sustained in the process of transnational migration? What are the gains and losses experienced by those who migrate? What are the variations in experience in respect of class, gender and generational dimensions? A general theme of transnationalism is the idea of 'globalisation from below', with groups of migrants viewed as creating and sustaining what Portes (2000) defines as 'transnational communities'. Elsewhere, Portes and Bach have described migration as a process of network building: "... which depends on and in turn reinforces social relations across space linking migrants and non-migrants" (1985, p 10). This perspective draws out the dynamic nature of the ties maintained through different stages of migration. Westwood and Phizacklea emphasise the "active decision-making processes of migration and the ways in which economic and cultural phenomena are creatively reinscribed in new settings and the ways in which the diasporic feeds economically and culturally back into the homeland, for instance, through remittances" (2000, p 7).

While studies of migration, colonisation and class have formed an important context for understanding ethnicity (Brah, 1996), they have also frequently understated gender. For example, much of the analysis of migration assumed a model either of family migration led by men, or of male pioneers followed by female and younger dependants. Papastergiadis, in his study *The turbulence of migration*, develops this point:

> The ... feminization of migration is a growing trend that was overlooked in the early literature. The stereotypical image of the migrant as the 'male urban peasant' reflected the mass migrations to the industrial centres of the west in the post-war period. However, this image has little resonance in the context of globalisation with its more turbulent and dispersed streams of movement. The literature on migration must now concern itself more with the relationship between gender and mobility. By focusing on male entry into industrial projects, theorists have not noticed the arrival of women through family migration schemes, and also their key role in the service industries. (2000, p 62)

Bangladeshi women have also been a neglected group, with some of the early oral histories in this area (notably, Adams, 1987; Choudhury, 1993) focusing exclusively on men. Yet women migrants play a distinctive role within transnational communities. Khanum highlights their economic role in strengthening kinship ties (often to the detriment of their own needs). She observes:

> [The] kinship tie demands that women send money to the poor relatives of their husbands in Bangladesh. Apart from these cases, women also have to contribute to relatives living in the UK even when they are supported by the Social Security department or from their own earnings, simply because of the prevailing norms. (1994, p 296)

Women also play a crucial role in the construction of what Hochschild refers to as 'global care chains', these representing the "personal links between people across the globe based on the paid or unpaid work of caring" (2000, p 131).

Migration may, on the other hand, bring major new opportunities for women. Westwood and Phizacklea (2000, p 108) refer to it as providing an economic and social escape route. While DeLaet poses the question: *"Does international migration provide women with an opportunity for liberating themselves from subordinate gender roles in their countries of origin, or are traditional gender roles perpetuated in the host societies?"* (1999, p 2, emphasis added).

The question raised by DeLaet is especially apt in relation to the women reported in this study, who may experience a complex interaction between feelings of liberation on the one side, and those of oppression on the other. Vertovec makes the point that: "Following migration the position of women in families and in the wider community often undergoes considerable transformation" (2000, p 15). Ethnicity, interacting with gender, may, however, become a source of positive rather than stigmatised identity. Barot et al (1999) argue that insofar as young women are concerned, they may play a major role in refusing to see themselves and their cultures as 'inferior' or 'alien'. They suggest that the 'second generation' in Britain has been engaged with reconceptualising and deconstructing ethnicity. Barot et al conclude that:

> This has involved disaggregating notions of 'black' and 'white' to explore the situation of women in particular ethnic categories, and also presenting aspects of culture disparaged by White feminists (arranged marriages, wearing the veil) within a framework that treats difference as positive and queries the view of Western gender arrangements as being more progressive. (1999, p 19)

By contrast, non-UK born women may have contradictory experiences in relation to reconstructing identity, especially given pressures within the home and family. This was brought out in Khanum's (1994) research on Bangladeshi women living in a small district of Manchester. She argued that the economic security created by migration had come at the cost of social status within the home and family. Although the position of women in Bangladesh is certainly precarious, Khanum (p 108) notes the crucial role they play in agriculture and productive activities within the home, citing data showing a female participation rate in agriculture of 54%. She goes on to argue:

> [In] ... rural Bangladesh women are the key members of a family in terms of class and position. When the women who played this key role in the social sphere on their own at home, migrated to the UK they found themselves in a new sphere of life and society where they have very little to do with the family, social and economic fields. Although the regular receipts from Social Security inflate family income ... they fail to bring financial liberty and self-esteem. In the majority of cases their rights are not established on these receipts because the money is being handled by husbands and fathers-in-law. These women have been alienated even from the money meant for themselves. Except for a few, the majority of the women experience a sense of isolation and insecurity in spite of their secure economic life in England. (1994, p 109)

In contrast, female migrants may also be viewed as 'active agents', making important decisions for and on behalf of their families (Westwood and Phizacklea, 2000). Migration may also have a significant impact on social identity, raising questions such as: how is identity maintained/reinvented in the new homeland? To what extent are there major changes in the way in which women define themselves in relation to home, family and working lives?

Further questions relate to issues concerning the internal structure of the family and the dynamics of family life. Combrinck-Graham (cited in Carter and McGoldrick, 1998) suggests 'centripetal' and 'centrifugal' forces operating on the family cycle. Centripetal forces relate to family closeness (for example, birth of a child), and centrifugal forces relate to separation (for example, children leaving home). Migration is characterised by a number of centrifugal forces, with people leaving their homeland, often in the early stages of family-building. This opens up boundaries between families and leads to the creation of what has been termed 'transnational families'. Periods of separation may be problematic, if occurring at a time when centripetal forces usually operate, with the migrant missing out

on large parts of the family cycle. One example is a male migrant returning home to Bangladesh to visit his wife, but failing to stay until the birth of his child. On the other hand, within the context of transnational families and globalisation, there are photographs, phone calls, video cameras and email, all of which aid participation in family life (Ho, 1991). Social networks may, therefore, be sustained in novel ways in transnational families, another important theme for investigation by this research. At the same time, first generation migrant women face the pressures associated with the move from a rural to an urban society, and from reconciling competing demands within the kinship system. These issues are explored in different ways in the section reporting the empirical findings from our research.

Research on Bangladeshi women

Although research on the Bangladeshi community has greatly expanded in recent years, work in relation to women remains a neglected area[1]. The experiences of younger Bangladeshis have been the subject of a number of projects (see, for example, Eade, 1997b; Gavron, 1997; Desai, 2000), and the lives of older people have been examined by Gardner (2002), Qureshi (1998) and Phillipson et al (2001). Family and household issues have been explored in important doctoral research from Khanum (1994, 2001) working in Manchester, and Pollen (2002) in the Bethnal Green district of Tower Hamlets.

However, the lives of adult Bengali women, while invariably an important element in many studies (including those cited previously), has rarely been the focus for systematic research (Kabeer's, 2000, comparative study of homeworkers in Bangladesh and Tower Hamlets being one of the few exceptions). On the other hand, the context and character of migration experienced by Bangladeshi women undoubtedly raises some important sociological and social policy issues. Migration by Sylheti women was itself long delayed. Ballard (2001) notes that women of Sylheti origin were rarely seen in Britain until the

---

[1] Research on Bangladeshis was brought together in 2002 at London Guildhall University in a two-day conference: *Bangladeshis in Britain: changes and choices, configurations and perspectives.*

early 1980s. Their appearance over the next two decades can be attributed to a variety of factors, including changes in immigration controls, improved facilities (mosques, *madrasas* and *halal* butchers) within the Bengali/Muslim community, the need of husbands for care and support, and greater instability within Bangladesh itself (Gardner, 2002). Gardner emphasises the importance of what she refers to as the "increasing Islamicization of British space over the 1970s and 1980s" (2002, p 109). She comments that:

> Increasingly, specific areas of Britain were becoming viable places in which to be a Muslim. In Tower Hamlets, for example, not only is the East London mosque a striking example of Middle Eastern architecture, but with its prominent position on the Whitechapel Road, and the broadcast of its *azan* (call to prayer), it is a graphic claim to British space by local Muslims. (2002, pp 109-10)

The arrival of women in the community, however, immediately raised a number of issues. In the first place, those moving to London (and Tower Hamlets in particular) faced major problems in a housing market that offered few options for couples on low incomes with a large number of children. The women had to further adapt to coping with a complex health and social care system, for themselves, their husbands and their children, while lacking familiarity with English. This had to be managed within the context of handling the move from a "rural peasant society to a hostile urban culture" (Kabeer, 2000, p 282), one which required major adjustments for the women involved.

A second factor was that the women migrated at a point when the family in Bangladesh, and in particular relationships between women and men, was itself undergoing change. The economic and political crises of the 1970s, and the decline of family-based farming in particular, had eroded traditional gender roles. Kabeer (2000, p 140) refers to the resulting erosion of the "patriarchal contract, and the increased inability of men to sustain the model of the male breadwinner". The consequence of this was a more general challenge to the family system itself:

> The loss of faith in the traditional patriarchal family to safeguard women's interests and to secure their

future expressed by many of the women workers ... appears to be part of a much more widespread anxiety and bitterness expressed by women in Bangladesh. Statistical estimates of divorce, male abandonment, marital instability and female-headed households do not come close to capturing how widespread the loss of faith appears to be. With the manifest failure, or inability, on the part of so many men to 'deliver' their side of the patriarchal bargain, it is not surprising that so many women were looking back on the choices that their parents had made on their behalf, on the life chances which these choices had given them and questioning whether it had been enough. (Kabeer, 2000, p 180)

Such reflections on the part of women were to be tested in a different way in the process of migration. Gardner makes the point that many of the women in her sample in Tower Hamlets had been "... 'sent for' by their husbands because they were growing old and needed someone to care for them" (2002, p 109). But this might be viewed as a further point of pressure on the contract between husband and wife, especially given the financial difficulties likely to be experienced by many families. This has to be placed within the context of a third issue of relevance to female migrants; namely the possibility of their experiencing what Becker (1997) refers to as 'disrupted lives', or lives separated from meaningful routines and traditions. From the earlier study of older male migrants from Bangladesh, the experience of discontinuity over the life course had been observed as an important element of their daily lives (Phillipson et al, 2001). In a more general sense, it might be argued that the experience of migration challenges traditional life course models which conceptualise a linear development from birth to death through education, work and retirement (Hoerder, 2001). Becker develops this point:

> Although continuity is apparently a human need and a universal expectation across cultures, continuity has a culture-specific shape. Western ideas about the course of life emphasize linearity. Metaphoric images of development and progress include gain and loss. The life span is seen as hierarchical, and aging as a 'hill'. The underlying assumption that development occurs over the entire course of life has its roots in long-standing theories of evolution that inform notions of order and progress in the West. Western thought is organized to make sense of individual lives

as orderly projects, but when this concept of the life course is translated into experiences of individual people, there is a great deal of slippage because real lives are more unpredictable than the cultural ideal. (1997, p 5)

This last point may be especially relevant to migrants who may experience complex transitions and disruptions over what may be crucial periods of the life course (for example, around marriage, the birth of children or widowhood). More generally, it is important to consider the type of insecurities generated through a chaotic and disrupted life course, and the attempts people may make to restore a sense of order and control to their world. This itself may be a strongly gendered process, with important contrasts between women and men in the way in which disorder is managed and controlled.

Conclusion

The aim of this chapter has been to provide a summary of the background to the research, and to consider the range of existing knowledge about Bangladeshis in Britain. The chapter has also introduced the idea of transnational migration; a concept that is referred to at different points in this report. The Bangladeshi women studied here have been (mostly) long-term residents of Tower Hamlets. They have retained, however, significant transnational ties and these are likely to have an important impact on daily life. More generally, on the basis of national surveys, women in the 35-55 age group are likely to have a range of roles and responsibilities within and beyond the immediate household. This research represents the first systematic investigation into the issues and concerns facing this significant group within the South Asian community. The next chapter of this report discusses the methodological approach adopted by the research and reviews the research questions explored in the empirical investigation of the lives of women migrants from Bangladesh.

2

Methodology of the study

This chapter examines a variety of methodological issues tackled by the study in pursuit of its research objectives. Studying the lives of Bangladeshi women presented a number of challenges. The target group was almost certainly likely to be first generation (non-English speaking) migrants who might have some reservations about the purpose and value of social research. Moreover, at a community level, we were working within a locality that had already been investigated in numerous studies over the post-war period, some of which had begun to include different groups within the Bangladeshi population (Eade, 1997a, 1997b; Gavron, 1997; Gardner, 1998; Pollen, 2002). In addition, there were questions concerning access to a representative population, about the type of data to be collected, and the range of contacts that needed to be developed with relevant local organisations. This chapter focuses on describing the key decisions in respect of entering the field and collecting and analysing the data. We also briefly reflect on some of the issues to be considered in interviewing the group of women who were the focus for the research. The chapter begins, however, with a brief introduction to the setting for the research, the London Borough of Tower Hamlets, home to the largest community of Bangladeshis in the UK.

The research setting

The context for the research study is of particular importance. The size and character of the Bangladeshi community in Tower Hamlets is an important element in this research. As noted in the previous chapter, nearly one in two Bangladeshis in the UK reside in inner London, with Tower Hamlets having the largest proportion of these. John Eade refers to the fact that the area has emerged as "... the political and cultural dynamo of [a] rapidly expanding British Bengali population" (1997a, p 94). But the community has a number of histories and experiences that form a powerful background to the study. On the one hand, there is the history of successive waves of migration into the area – Huguenots, Polish and Russian Jews, Maltese, Cypriots, Chinese, Bengalis and Somalis. On the other hand, there is the story of the extended family embedded within a working-class community (explored in studies such as those by Townsend, 1957 and Young and Willmott, 1957). These distinctions retain some physical significance in the area between Shoreditch and Aldgate, which contains the majority of the Bangladeshi community, and Docklands wards such as St Katherine's and Millwall, which remain predominantly white.

These histories are important in that they suggest at least two different traditions of relevance to the research. First, a community that has for centuries been a reception point for those fleeing political oppression, seeking economic betterment or those settling for an urban existence (Widgery, 1991). This aspect of community life has allowed a variety of migrant networks to flourish, supported by shops, religious centres and festivals – the trappings associated with a cultural, as well as a social and economic presence. This dimension is essentially about efforts to develop a sense of 'inclusion', even for groups who may experience living on the margins of urban life. The second tradition, however, is the response of 'insiders' (to use a term from community sociology) to the presence of new migrant groups (Crow et al, 2001). Studies such as those from Cornwell (1984) and Phillipson et al (2001) have highlighted the extent of racism in the area and the threats directed at Bangladeshis, in particular, by their white neighbours. These aspects must themselves be placed against a background of poverty, poor housing and increasing social and economic divisions affecting the area (symbolised by the gentrification of some parts and the increasingly squalid nature of others).

Both of these traditions are of relevance to the study. On the one hand, the extent to which first generation migrant women have reconstructed and adapted social networks within the area will be explored. Such networks almost certainly move well beyond the geographical borders of Tower Hamlets, stretching to Bangladeshi communities in the UK and elsewhere, and of course to Bangladesh itself. On the other hand, the immediate area has a powerful presence influencing the extent to which people feel able to control and to some degree influence their immediate social environment. Both these dimensions are important in assessing the response of the women in the research in making the transition from rural to urban lifestyles.

The consultation phase

The initial phase of the research set out to inform existing contacts within Tower Hamlets about the study and to seek new sources of potential help and advice. This process was pursued in three main ways: first, through the establishment of a group to advise on the development of the research; second, raising awareness within the community about the study; and third, through preliminary work for the pilot phase of the research. The activities associated with each are now summarised before examining the implementation phase of the study. Establishing a local advisory group proved to be of considerable benefit as the work progressed. The role of the group – both in meetings and through individual advice – was to provide suggestions about helpful contacts, to provide a sounding board on methodological issues, to comment on the development of the questionnaire, and to advise on ethical and policy issues raised by the study. An initial task of the group was to review the research questions underpinning the project. These were formulated in the following way:

- What is the position of Bangladeshi women aged 35-55 within the household and the wider kinship group?
- What is the range of activities of this group within and beyond the extended family?
- How are expectations about social roles changing among different generations of women?
- What are the migration and biographical experiences of Bangladeshi women?
- What issues are faced by women in providing care and support?
- What evidence is there for isolation and social exclusion from the wider community?
- What is the role of external agencies (carers groups, religious organisations, statutory bodies) in providing assistance to these women?
- What policy innovations will be needed to provide help and support to Bangladeshi women in their role as carers within multigenerational households?

Following the establishment of the advisory group, the next task was to raise awareness about the project within Tower Hamlets. This was tackled in two main ways. First, leaflets were produced and distributed to a range of organisations within the borough (see Appendix A). These were produced both in Bengali and English, and summarised the main aims of the work, as well as inviting anyone interested to contact the research worker for the study. As Sylheti is a spoken dialect with no written form, special efforts were made to keep the language as simple as possible. Drafts of the leaflet were piloted on groups of women to ensure the information was easily understandable. Second, contact was made with key organisations within the local area, the purpose being to talk to them about the projected research and to gather any views they might have on how they could contribute to the research.

Organisations involved in assisting the research at various points over the next two years were:

- *Tower Hamlets Parents Centre.* This organisation provides education and support to parents throughout the borough, both at the centre and through outreach classes at schools within the borough. The centre provided participants for one of the focus groups and pre-pilot and pilot interviews. The centre manager also joined the consultancy group for the study.

- *Jagonari Women's Centre.* This is a well-established organisation with a variety of activities and courses aimed at Bangladeshi women of all ages. The research worker for this project was invited to join the management team of the centre.
- *APASENTH.* This is an advice and support group for Asian people with disabilities and special needs. For the first phase of exploratory interviews, the organisation provided access to women involved in informal care to assist with framing relevant questions to this group.
- *Graduates' Forum.* This organisation operates an agency to promote the skills of Bangladeshi graduates living in Tower Hamlets. The forum arranged for a number of their clients to participate in one of the focus groups comprising young Bangladeshi women.
- *St Dunstan's Resource Centre.* Located on the Ocean Estate in Stepney, this centre provides a wide range of activities for the community. Members of the staff participated in a young women's focus group.
- *Mulberry Girls' School.* This school was attended by many of the daughters of the women interviewed for the study and provided a focus group from its class of sixth formers.

Other organisations were also contacted both to raise the profile of the study and to gain advice from community workers. These organisations included:

- *Dame Colet House.* Located within the Ocean Estate in Stepney, this organisation provides a range of activities for the community, many targeted at women.
- *Social Action for Health.* This group brings together a number of community health projects with a particular focus on the Bangladeshi community.
- *Bromley-by-Bow Centre.* This organisation runs a number of courses and schemes aimed at women, which are designed to introduce them to a wide range of skills.

Contact with organisations was complemented by discussions with individual workers from social service organisations, general practitioners, health workers and university academics with an interest in researching ethnic minority groups.

The pre-pilot and pilot study

Based on comments from the advisory group and the various organisations listed previously, it was decided to design a questionnaire that would collect specific pieces of information about the women, but that would also allow them to talk more generally about their everyday lives and relationships. To gain an idea of the kind of issues that would need to be included, a limited number of pre-pilot interviews were conducted where the agenda was set by the interviewee. From this material, a more formalised pilot study was conducted consisting of focus groups with middle and younger generation women, as well as 12 interviews with individual respondents.

Focus groups with the target age group of women were held at Tower Hamlets Parents Centre and Jagonari Women's Centre. Contact was established with the women at both organisations before they were invited to participate in the groups. Following analysis of the focus group data, a draft questionnaire was devised for the pilot interviews. Twelve in-depth individual interviews were conducted: four at the respondents' homes, six at the Parents Centre, and two at APASENTH. The length of the interviews ranged from one to two hours. Ten of the interviews were held with women aged 35-55, and two with women aged 21 and 60. The latter were included to provide comparison with early and recent migrants. All of the women had children and four were widows. The mean age of the women was 43 years and 9 months. They had lived in the UK between 1–30 years, with a mean of 15 years and 4 months.

The interviews provided information about the lives of the women, including their day-to-day activities, as well as more life changing events, such as marriage and migration. The women spoke of their initial reactions to coming to the UK, and how they had adapted to their new life and to their local community in particular. Following the individual interviews, a focus group with Bangladeshi women aged 21-23 years was carried out to compare and contrast experiences with the older generation of women. The pilot work was subject to analysis and discussion within the research team and written-up as a project working paper (Ahmed et al, 2001). This resulted in a number of key themes being identified for selection in the final questionnaire. These included:

- Migration histories and their impact on adjustment to life in the UK.
- Household structure and responsibilities.
- Changing Muslim, Sylheti, Bengali, Bangladeshi and British identities.
- Relationships with younger generations.
- Financial and housing circumstances.
- Mental and physical health status.
- Work and employment histories.

These topics were developed into a draft questionnaire that was circulated for discussion with the consultancy group and other organisations and individuals. The final questionnaire combined a mix of pre-coded and open-ended questions exploring the above themes (see Appendix B). In spring 2000, the projected study, along with a draft of the questionnaire, was submitted to the East London and the City Health Authority Research Ethics Sub-Committee for approval. At this stage, the sub-committee raised a number of concerns about the recruitment process, the nature of the questions to be asked, and the method of approaching subjects. The proposal was re-submitted and received final approval in November 2000.

Preparing for the main survey

Following approval for the study from the Ethics Committee, a number of options were considered for recruiting subjects to the study. The desired option was to use the age-sex registers of general practitioners in the borough. However, other possibilities were also considered, including using lists of women in the relevant age groups involved in organisations such as those collaborating with the project (see previously). Another idea was drawing a sample from the lists of tenants of local authority housing. The disadvantage of these and other ideas concerned the likelihood of important groups being missed or under-represented. In contrast, evidence from community health surveys suggest that most Bangladeshis in the target age group (35-55) were likely to be registered with a general practitioner and this still seemed the best source for recruiting subjects. Having settled on using age-sex registers, 17 health centres and/or single-handed general practitioners were approached, with seven of these eventually agreeing to take part. These were spread fairly evenly around the borough, taking in Bethnal

Green, Bow, Mile End, Poplar, Shoreditch, Spitalfields, Stepney, Whitechapel and Wapping. The Docklands and Isle of Dogs areas were under-represented because of the lack of participating general practitioners.

The practices provided lists of all Bangladeshi women aged 35-55 who were registered with them. From these a random list (using every fifth name) was drawn, generating 220 names of women who were subsequently invited to take part in the study. Recruitment was undertaken in two main stages. For the first stage, respondents were sent a letter giving them information about the study. This was followed up by a telephone call where further information concerning the research was provided, any questions were answered and where a visit to the respondent's house was arranged. Letters were sent in both Bengali and English. This ensured that if the targeted individual had literacy problems there would be someone in the house able to read the correspondence and explain it to them. At this stage of recruitment it was found that incorrect details had been provided for 66 of the 220. These came under the headings of incorrect telephone number, no telephone number or other erroneous details (usually that the person had moved away from the property or that the person was not known at the property). Where there was a problem with the telephone number, follow-up letters were sent, which included a tear-off slip to return where the respondent could indicate whether they were interested in participating in the research. Removing those with incorrect details and concentrating only on those who had received a telephone call and/or had been sent a follow-up letter reduced the potential sample to 154 respondents.

From these respondents 100 women agreed to participate in the study (giving a response rate of 65%). Of the remaining 54, 28 women refused, saying that they were either not interested or too busy. There were 13 respondents where someone else (usually a member of the family) had refused on behalf of the women – in some cases after they had agreed to participate in the research. A further 13 women were unavailable to be seen: five were in Bangladesh; four said that their health was too poor; three were caring for other family members; and in one case the respondent's mother had recently died.

The 100 women eventually recruited were evenly distributed across the different age bands: 29 were between 35-39; 29 were between 40-44; 21 were aged 45-49; and 21 were aged between 50-55. Seventy-six of the women were married; 17 widowed; and seven were separated or divorced. The average family size for the sample was 5.2 children; 66% had five or more children.

Finally, following completion of the 100 interviews, two focus groups were conducted with women from younger age groups. One consisted of girls aged 16-18 years drawn from the sixth form of a local school; the other a group of women in their twenties who were working in the borough of Tower Hamlets. These discussions, along with the previous focus group of young women aged 21-23, provided contrasting views from a younger generation about the issues of concern to the study.

Interviewing Bangladeshi women

All the respondents were interviewed in their homes, with the average length of each interview lasting approximately one hour. Ninety-six interviews were conducted in Sylheti, three partly in English and partly in Sylheti, and one wholly in English. Cooperation from the respondent was rated as 'good or very good' in 84 cases, and 'poor or very poor' in three cases. In 51 cases someone else was present during the interview (usually a husband or children). In six cases it was felt that the presence of others might have influenced responses a 'fair amount' or a 'great deal'. In a further 14 cases it was recorded as probably 'just a little'. These assessments have to be examined from a number of perspectives. In the first place, conducting a one-to-one interview (with no one else present in the room) was difficult to secure given the extent of overcrowding in many of the homes (an average of 1.518 persons per room, excluding kitchen and bathroom). Interviews, even if timed after children had gone to school, would often be interrupted by someone in the home (a husband, relative, sick child) or someone calling at the house. These are of course the normal hurdles characteristic of research in community settings, but they are especially acute in complex as opposed to single-person households. This environmental context needs to be kept in mind when assessing and interpreting the data. It had a significant impact on

certain types of questions with, for example, responses about marriage certainly being conditioned by the presence of husbands and/or children either in the room or the household (in 21 cases overall).

Another important issue concerns the process of interviewing as experienced by the respondents. In a number of respects, this was an especially challenging group. Paul Corrigan (1979) has made the point, in a study of teachers and pupils in a comprehensive school, that for people to talk about themselves (to a complete stranger) for an hour or more may be somewhat unusual. Interviews conducted for social science research may therefore conflict with normal biographical experience. This observation is especially relevant to the women in the sample, whose own stories and experiences were often marginalised in the routine of household life.

Another issue concerned the religious dimension to the lives of the women interviewed. Most identified being Muslim as a central part of their identity, and the importance of this in respect of sustaining meaning and continuity in daily life should be noted. On the other hand, it also raised issues within the interview: 'only Allah knows' was a not uncommon response to probes on different questions, one that would often limit further questioning. And the pressure on some of the women also created difficulties: "just think what I could have done [how much housework] whilst talking to you [the interviewer] ...", was the comment from one respondent, indicating her preoccupation with concerns other than a study of migrant women. But these negative observations should also be balanced by the extent to which respondents talked, often in a moving and frank way, about the nature of their daily lives, their ties with Bangladesh and their aspirations for the future. These responses form much of what is said in this report and provide the basis for the policy recommendations that are set out in the final chapter.

Interviews for the study were carried out for much of 2001, with additional fieldwork completed in early 2002. The bulk of interviews were conducted by the Sylheti-speaking research worker employed for the research project. In all cases, the interviews were tape-recorded and subsequently transcribed from Sylheti to English. The transcriptions were read in detail by the research team and codes developed for the open-ended questions. The analysis developed in subsequent chapters combines both a summary of the pre-coded and post-coded data (using the statistical package SPSSx), and use of the software package WinMax to explore responses to the open-ended questions. All names have been changed to protect the anonymity of the interviewees, and further information is given where relevant.

Conclusion

The purpose of this chapter has been to summarise the various stages of the research undertaken prior to entry into the field. An important issue arising from this is the need for careful negotiation within different community-based agencies, notably around the question of explaining the purpose of the research and for seeking help and information. In this context, the kind of work undertaken (as with all social research) does rest on observing certain rules and procedures when entering the field, and for negotiating access to resources of various kinds. These issues are, however, especially important in the context of research on minority ethnic groups, where linguistic and cultural barriers may also need to be overcome. In this context, some guidelines (see Appendix C) have been identified for researchers undertaking the kind of study developed for this project, and the concluding chapter of this study returns to a discussion of the background to some of these points.

3

Migration and the family life of Bangladeshi women

The 1960s witnessed a significant expansion in the population of Bangladeshis living in Britain. The historical roots of this ethnic minority group have already been noted in Chapter One, but the pioneers were joined by a new wave of male migrants (during the 1960s and early 1970s) and subsequently by their wives and dependants. In the space of 30 years the population of Bangladeshis in Britain grew from around 6,000 to approaching 163,000. By 1981, there were some 10,000 Bangladeshis resident in Tower Hamlets and by the close of the 20th century that number had grown to around 60,000. The growth of the Bangladeshi community has been reviewed, from a historical perspective, in studies such as those by Adams (1987) and Choudhury (1993). John Eade (1999) suggests, however, that our knowledge about the experiences of the first generation remains patchy, and this is especially true of the women who started to arrive in increasing numbers from villages in Sylhet from the late 1970s onwards. This chapter examines the experience of migration and goes on to consider the household structure and family relationships among our sample of women.

Migration and city life

Peter Ackroyd points out that London has always been a city of immigrants[1]. He cites the remark of an observer in the mid–18th century: "... when I consider this great city, in its several quarters, or divisions, I look upon it as an aggregate of various nations, distinguished from each other by their respective customs, manners, and interests" (2000, p 701). Ackroyd (2001) cites elsewhere an old German proverb: 'City air makes you free', and the possibility of establishing a new life is the magnet that invariably draws people to urban centres. Katy Gardner (1995, p 62), in her study of rural Bangladesh, notes the 'transformative powers' ascribed to the lands to which people aspire. She cites the image of London held by two non-migrants, talking in the late 1980s:

London (ie the UK) is a good, beautiful place. There, all types of food are available. In Bangladesh nothing is available. In London, everyone is happy.

In London, everybody's rich, and there's no fighting. Everything is clean, too: there is no mud like here. (1995, p 62)

Gavron's (1997) study of young Bangladeshi women in Bethnal Green identifies a number of reasons for the growing numbers of Bangladeshi women entering the UK in the early 1970s. She cites the political and social fall-out from the war of liberation with Pakistan (in 1971) as one major factor, with the resulting increase in the number of people left destitute and landless (a finding confirmed in Hartmann and Boyce's, 1979, work in Bangladesh in the 1970s). Domestically, successive immigration Acts in Britain had begun to erect obstacles to further migration. The 1971 Immigration Act, to take one example, continued to allow the entry of 'dependants' of men already in Britain, but with an age limit of 18 or under in the case of children. Gavron suggests that:

---

[1] This is especially true of the East End of London, an aspect examined in different ways by Roy Porter (1994) and Peter Ackroyd (2001).

This was the trigger for the arrival of a number of the families coming in the late 1970s and early 1980s: for the men who had first come to Britain in the early 1960s and married in the few years afterwards, these were the years when their older children were reaching the age of 18, after which they would no longer be allowed into Britain. (1997, p 55)

Gavron also notes the influence of the 1968 Commonwealth Immigration Act, which laid down that dependent children could only come to join their fathers in Britain if accompanied by their mothers:

If the sons of migrant workers were going to follow their fathers in seeking work in Britain, in effect this meant that whole families had to come to Britain: sons could not come if over 18, if under 18 they could not come without their mothers, and girls would have to accompany their mothers and brothers if they could not be left with other kin in Bangladesh. (1997, p 55)

Our sample of 100 women left Bangladesh in their mid-twenties (mean age 25.6 years) and had lived in Britain for an average of nearly 18 years. Twenty-nine per cent had been in Britain for 20 or more years, making them representative of some of the early arrivals in the 1970s and 1980s. However, the large proportion coming from their late teens through to early adulthood is significant. Most had well-established family and social networks within their village in Sylhet. For them, migration was an economic gamble, but it had social dimensions as well. Gardner suggests that migration can be seen as "part of a wider project in which individuals and households strive to reinvent themselves" (1995). But for young women – often the least powerful within communities – this can be a daunting experience. Nalia Kabeer's (2000) research on Bangladeshi women in Tower Hamlets records the pressure on first generation immigrants in trying to adjust to a new and different life. She concludes that:

We see evidence in the London testimonies of the stresses involved in making the adjustment from a slow-moving, rural society in one of the poorest countries in the world to the fast-paced urban life in one of the richer ones. The normal process of transition involved in international migration was made immeasurably more difficult by the shock of

contrast between the two different cultural milieus. (2000, p 268)

What were some of the recollections about the impact of migration from the women in this study? Nearly two thirds (62%) recalled feelings of sadness about leaving their home and family, although this was often linked to a sense of the 'inevitability' of joining a husband and completing the family unit:

"It feels very bad to leave your family behind. But you have to come for your own family don't you?" (Sultana, arrived 1980)

"I had to come here to be with my husband. He lived and worked here … so that's why I had to come." (Shamima, arrived 1983)

"How could I feel? I left all my family behind – my mother, my father, my brothers. It felt bad. But I came. I couldn't really not come could I? My husband was here. I worried a lot for my family … I missed them." (Salma, arrived 1977)

Coming as young wives, still in their teens or early twenties, it was the strangeness of settling into London that most could recall. Few of the respondents (just 9%) came from urban areas: most were rural migrants entering one of the biggest and most densely populated cities in the world. Not surprisingly, over one third (35%) mentioned feelings of initial isolation:

"I felt very lonely. Anyone would feel like that if they went to a new country wouldn't they? I couldn't speak the language and I couldn't understand anyone around me when I went out." (Saleha, arrived 1982)

"When I went out it felt strange because I couldn't make any sense of anything around me. I couldn't understand anything anyone said." (Aklisun, arrived 1985)

"At first it was a bit scary. Things like electricity – I didn't understand it. There were so many new things. I was scared of being so alone. My husband wasn't there all the time. It was just me and the young children. I was worried because I didn't know how I would get on. I couldn't speak English. I didn't know how I would manage. If an English person came to the door what would I say? What if they came in and killed me?" (Rupa, arrived 1983)

"It was difficult for me. I couldn't speak the language so I couldn't go out. I was scared of going out with my children. What if something happened and we got lost, how would we get back?" (Dina, arrived 1985)

For some, it was London itself that failed to measure up to expectations:

"It wasn't the way I had expected it to be. In Bangladesh, we can't imagine what it will be like. I didn't like it. I had thought it would be wonderful, but it wasn't. As soon as I left the airport I said to my sister and her husband: 'What is this? I heard London was such a wonderful place. What is this?' They said, 'wait till you get inside London, you will see what it is really like'. But even when I came home it was nothing special. I had heard so much about London, and it was nothing like what I expected. People always talk about how great London is, but when I came, I realised there was nothing great about it." (Fultara, arrived 1981)

The shock of experiencing a different climate was an issue mentioned by a number of the women:

"When we first came here, the whole first week it snowed very heavily. It was about a foot deep. I had never seen snow before. I thought 'what kind of country is this?' It was very cold." (Yasmeen, arrived 1987)

"The first day I came here it was a very dark day. I didn't like it from then. And the cold was unbearable. I didn't go out. I had never seen anything like this country. I didn't like it." (Fazira, arrived 1979)

"It felt so bad! I came in November and it was really very cold. I didn't like it at all. My husband was at work all the time. He would work from the morning through to the night, so I was on my own a lot." (Jusna, arrived 1980)

On the other hand, it is important to note those who were happy to leave Bangladesh and who had positive expectations about coming to Britain. In some cases there was the satisfaction of re-establishing contact with close family members:

"This is a nice country. I liked it. I had found my sister again after so long. I was very happy." (Hafiza, arrived 1993)

"It was nice. I was seeing my sister who I hadn't seen for a long time." (Tahera, arrived 1993)

"I liked it. I found a lot of relatives I hadn't seen for a long time." (Amina, arrived 1989)

Others mentioned the benefits of leaving a country racked with hunger and poverty:

"I was happy to leave. We live in a poor country, why should I boast about it and say that it was such a great place to live and I was sorry to leave? I was coming from a poor country to a rich one, of course I was happy to leave." (Teraful, arrived 1977)

"I was happy to come. Ours is a poor country." (Jolikha, arrived 1991)

The women came to the UK, as noted in Chapter One, not as individual migrants but as members of transnational communities and households. In this sense, comments about the experience of isolation need to be placed within a wider context. Roger Ballard (2001) makes the point that the vast majority of migrants move along what he refers to as 'increasingly well-worn paths', built around networks of reciprocity maintained through kinship. Moreover, he suggests that migrant flows tend to be highly concentrated both in terms of the sending villages and the receiving urban centres. The women in the study confirm this view: 51% came from just three districts in Sylhet – Bishwanath, Balaganj and Jagganatpur. And the area of first residence in the UK was equally concentrated. The majority headed straight for the East End of London (10 of the women went initially to Aldgate, a focus for help and support for new arrivals from Bangladesh dating back at least to the 1930s)[2]. Although a small number of women came to the UK alone, most came with husbands and/or husbands and children. A majority

---

[2] Interestingly, one of David Widgery's Jamaican respondents, recalling his entry into London after disembarking from the *Empire Windrush*, comments: "To find another coloured man I had to go to Aldgate East" (1991, p 197).

then spent an initial period at least with other members from their kin and village network:

"We stayed with a family that my husband knew from before; later we got our own place." (Suleya, arrived 1979)

"We stayed with my brother for two years." (Habiba, arrived 1982)

"We were at my husband's cousin's house. I met a lot of his family in the first few weeks!" (Fahima, arrived 1985)

"Just someone from our village. I called him uncle. We were new and didn't know anyone." (Nazma, arrived 1991)

For the women in this study, migration from Bangladesh to Britain formed one element in a complex period of transition, with different moves and changes of status. Marriage was one part of this, with virtually all of those interviewed (there were four exceptions) having been married in Sylhet. There was then a varying period of time – from a matter of weeks to a period of a year or more – before settlement in the UK. In between this, children might be born, husbands would make visits back and forth and relationships would be established with new in-laws. Following migration, there were then a number of moves around London and the East End (mainly the latter), sometimes involving temporary accommodation (in hotels or staying with relatives) before moving (usually) to accommodation rented from the local authority:

"First we came to my mother's house for a day and then the next day we went to a hotel…. We were in the hotel for one and a half years." (Jolikha, arrived 1991)

"At first we stayed with his sister for a little while and then we went to a hotel. We were there for about a year." (Rukshana, arrived 1987)

"As soon as we came we went to a hotel. We were there for nine months." (Nazmin, arrived 1987)

Wives coming to Tower Hamlets in the 1970s and 1980s faced a number of problems, especially in relation to housing and employment. Studies by Gavron (1997) and Pollen (2002) highlight the lack of affordable housing and the scarcity of accommodation suitable for meeting the needs of large families (discussed later). These difficulties were reinforced by the economic recession that coincided (and in some cases prompted) the move of established male migrants from towns in the north and the Midlands. The environment facing the new arrivals posed considerable difficulties, not least in terms of building and maintaining family and community life. However, before assessing some of the implications of this, the household and family structure of this sample of women is examined.

Bangladeshi households and family structure

We begin first with findings on the size of households, before examining issues about marriage and the relationships between the women and other household members. In the earlier description of the sample (see page 16), it was noted that among the women, 76% were married, 17% were widowed and 7% were divorced or separated. Census data has confirmed the relatively large size of Bangladeshi households – 5.3 persons in the 1991 Census (compared with 2.5 for the average household). Over 60% of Bangladeshi households were of five persons or more. In this study, the average household size was 6.6, and 87% of households comprised five or more persons: findings that reflect the particular age group targeted for the research. The 7% of households with 10 or more persons should also be noted; in contrast, there was just one single-person household. The average number of children was 5.2, with just 8% of women having two children or less (two women were childless). Two thirds of respondents had five or more children.

Eade et al (1996) describe Bangladeshi households as illustrating a conservative (traditional) pattern of nuclear and extended families, with relatively little manifestation of Western cohabitation. Our respondents confirm this observation, with a preponderance of nuclear families on the one hand and a number of complex multi-family households on the other. The nature of these households is such that some form of classification is helpful in delineating their main characteristics. In her analysis

of 175 households in the Bethnal Green/Globe
Town district of Tower Hamlets, Gavron (1997) (see
also Pollen, 2002) used the typology developed by
Kolenda (1968), and this has also been followed in
this research (see Table 3.1). Gavron's study is based
on a random survey of households out of which
those classified as Bangladeshi have been drawn.
Despite the more focused nature of our enquiry,
Table 3.1 suggests broad similarities between the two
surveys, at least on this measure of household
structure.

Table 3.1: Household structure

Type of family	Category	THS[a] %[c]	ICS[b] %[c]	Description
Nuclear family	I	59	61	A couple with or without unmarried children.
Supplemented nuclear family	II	4	2	A nuclear family plus one or more unmarried, separated or widowed relatives of the parents, other than their unmarried children.
Sub-nuclear family	III	17	20	A fragment of a former nuclear family. Typical examples are the widow or the widower with unmarried children or siblings – whether unmarried, widowed, separated or divorced – living together.
Single-person household	IV	1	2	
Supplemented sub-nuclear family	V	1	1	A group of relatives, members of a formerly complete nuclear family, plus some other unmarried, divorced or widowed relative who was not a member of the nuclear family; for example, a widow and her unmarried children plus her widowed mother-in-law.
Collateral joint family	VI	0	2	Two or more married couples between whom there is a sibling bond – usually a brother-brother relationship – plus unmarried children.
Supplemented collateral joint family	VII	3	3	A collateral joint family plus unmarried, divorced or widowed relatives. Typically, such supplemental relatives are the widowed mother of the married brothers, or the widower father, or an unmarried sibling.
Lineal joint family	VIII	14	9	Two couples between whom there is a lineal link, usually between parents and married son, sometimes between parents and married daughter.
Supplemented lineal joint family	IX	0	1	A lineal joint family plus unmarried, divorced, or widowed relatives who do not belong to either of the lineally linked nuclear families; for example, the father's widower brother or the son's wife's unmarried brother.
Lineal-collateral joint family	X	0	0	Three or more couples linked lineally and collaterally. Typically, parents and their two or more married sons, plus the unmarried children of the three or more couples.
Supplemented lineal-collateral joint family	XI	0	1	A lineal-collateral joint family plus unmarried, widowed or separated relatives who belong to none of the nuclear families lineally and collaterally linked; for example, the father's widowed sister or brother, or an unmarried nephew of the father.
Other	XII	1	1	
Total		**100**	**100**	

[a] Tower Hamlets Study
[b] Institute of Community Studies Survey (Gavron, 1997)
[c] Percentages may exceed 100 due to rounding up

To illustrate different household types, examples have been taken from the nuclear, sub-nuclear, lineal joint, and 'other' category. Taking two examples of nuclear families first of all:

> Sufia is aged 42 and came to the UK in 1981. She was married in Bangladesh in 1975 when she was 15. She came with her husband and two children (a boy and a girl); they have since had three further children – two boys and a girl. She has lived in her local authority flat since arriving in the UK. There are seven people in her household, including her spouse (aged 47) and her five children (aged 25, 22, 19, 17 and 13).
>
> Shumie is aged 36 and came to the UK when she was 16. She was married in Bangladesh in 1981 when she was 16 and came to the UK with her brother-in-law. She lives in a flat rented from the local authority. There are five people in her household, including her spouse (aged 45) and her three children (aged 15, 14 and 8).

Sub-nuclear families are illustrated by the following:

> Roshon is aged 40 and came to the UK when she was 30. She was married in Bangladesh in 1980 when she was 19 and came to the UK with her husband and four children. She lives in a flat rented from the local authority. Roshon's husband died of cancer in 2001. There are nine people in her household, including eight children (aged 20, 17, 15, 11, 7, 5, 18 months and 6 months).
>
> Rabia is aged 35 and came to the UK when she was 18. She was married in Bangladesh in 1980 when she was 14 and came to the UK with her husband and one child. She lives in a flat rented from the local authority. Rabia separated from her husband in 1997. There are six people in her household, including five children (aged 20, 15, 11, 10 and 4).

The following are two examples of lineal joint families:

> Beena is aged 45 and came to the UK when she was 34. She was married in Bangladesh in 1974 when she was 18 and came to the UK with her husband and three children. She lives in a flat rented from the local authority. There are eight people in her household, including Beena's spouse (aged 74), her five children (aged 23, 18, 17, 10 and 7) and a daughter-in-law.
>
> Teraful is aged 48 and came to the UK when she was 24. She was married in Bangladesh in 1968 when she was 14 and came to the UK with her husband and two children. She lives in a terraced house with her spouse. There are seven people in her household, including Teraful's spouse (aged 60), her three children (aged 28, 21 and 20), her son-in-law and a grandson (aged 8 months).

Finally, there is one household classified in category XII which illustrates the diversity of relationships encountered in some of the households:

> Zeba is aged 50 and came to the UK when she was 38. She was married in Bangladesh in 1973 when she was 22 and came to the UK on her own with her children. She lives in a terraced house with her children and the first wife of her late husband. There are ten people in her household, including her husband's first wife, three of her children (aged 26, 19, 15), two daughters-in-law, the son of her late husband and the first wife, a stepson and a grandson.

Household structure was itself influenced by restrictions on accommodation, an issue explored in the next chapter. For the moment, however, the next main objective of the research is considered; namely to explore the relationships between household members, in particular spouses and children.

Partners and children

All of the women in the study had managed and sustained relationships in a transnational context, variously with parents, husbands and children. Most, as already noted, had been married in Bangladesh and in many cases had their first children in that country. The majority of the women had begun one married life in the home of their new husband's family, with a period of separation from their husband in some cases soon after marriage. They then started another type of married life in a new home (usually after a succession of temporary homes) following migration to the UK. The average age at marriage for the women in the sample was 17.2 years, with 24% marrying at age 15 or below (two were married at the age of 12). Most of the women (86%) reported that their parents or an 'agent' ('middle-person') chose their spouse for them without their consent:

"Our parents arranged it. In those days we weren't even allowed to see the other person. There was more shame in those days." (Rafeya, married at 15)

"In our country nobody was asked for their consent when they got married. It wasn't needed because nobody would have objected." (Gulnehar, married at 17)

"I had an arranged marriage. When I was studying in class ten my father started looking for a good groom. At that time we had gained Independence – the Pakistani rule was over, and Bangladesh was independent. My father was initially very keen to get me married to a Bangladeshi groom ... he didn't want to get me married to anyone abroad. But then he saw that for someone with even a good job in Bangladesh, it was hard for them to maintain a family and wife. He was looking for the best for me, and he chose my husband. He saw that he [husband] had a good income – better than in Bangladesh. Then his family came and saw me and liked me – and we got married!" (Jusna, married at 17)

A number of respondents talked about the changes that marriage brought to their lives, especially with the move from the parental home:

"You have a lot more freedom at your parent's house don't you? After my marriage I had to behave myself a lot more! I had to be careful of what I said and did. And you have a lot more responsibility. You just grow up, don't you? You don't have a choice but to grow up." (Fazila, married at 20)

"All my freedom was gone. I had to ask them [husband's family] everything. If I wanted to go to

another room I had to ask them if I could go or not." (Asma, married at 17)

"It was a very big change! It took some time to get used to it. You change completely after your marriage. I got wise very quickly after I got married! I was very naïve before that! I don't know if everyone is like that. Maybe Allah gives some people all their wisdom in one go – but I got mine in small bits!" (Shumie, married at 16)

"When you go to your husband's village that is a brand new life isn't it? You have to leave your old life behind. In my father's house I had never even made a cup of tea! My mother was very young and active, she looked after our whole family without needing any of us to help. When I went to my husband's home I had to slowly learn by watching everyone else." (Ruji, married at 21)

Migration on the part of husbands would itself have been an important factor influencing these comments. Gulati's (1994) study *In the absence of their men* examined the impact of male migration on women living in the Indian state of Kerala. Gulati noted the dual effect on the lives of women: in the short term making them more dependent on close relatives (especially those of their new husbands); over the longer term, giving them more responsibilities for the running of the household. However, along with migration, marriage arrangements and the selection of partners also played a decisive role. Once again, the women reflected on a mixture of negative and positive experiences of the early years of marriage:

"It was a bit scary. I didn't have any sisters or even a sister-in-law, so there was no one to talk to me. I didn't know anything! When I got there I was so innocent! I came from a really small family, and in Bangladesh if you don't know how to manage a family then it is very hard [sighs deeply]. My husband's family was very big. It was very hard for me to try and get along with them all. My family is very small. There was just the three of us brothers and sisters and we had just the one cousin. And in my husband's family there were 35 people in the village." (Monwara, married at 16)

"At first I didn't like it. I was worried that I would never like them! But gradually I started to like them.

It is always hard when you move from one place to another." (Shumie, married at 16)

"I felt bad that I was getting married, because my friends weren't married and I was the first ... and I was also still in school and hadn't finished my studies. I felt bad generally that my parents were getting me married. Maybe I would have felt happy if I had been older, but because I was so young, I didn't really understand that I should be happy too. But I felt happy after my first child was born." (Saika, married at 16)

"It is because they didn't ask me that I have had so much difficulty in my life and I am here now. My parents arranged it. My marriage wasn't right. My father didn't know the truth. He [husband] went over and duped my father. He sent his relatives over and they hid so much of the truth. My father didn't know that he was living with an English woman here. I am one of a kind. No one else could bear what I have had to bear. My mother says, 'if it had been my older daughter in this marriage then she would have stabbed him by now. She would have got out any way she could'. That's what they say about my older sister. And they say about me 'this one is different'. They couldn't take me away even by trying. They told me to go back so many times. I said: 'You will take me back only to marry me off again, so why should I come back? What would that do for me? Will I be any happier?' So that's why I didn't go back. I always hoped that he would change, but he never did." (Fultara, married at 19; separated at 41)

"My sister arranged the marriage. She thought he was a good man. But I couldn't stay with him. He used to beat me and he was very greedy. He was a gambler and drinker and he took drugs. He didn't want to work. He always sent me to my brothers and sisters to get money from them, and if I didn't get money he would beat me. Then I couldn't take it anymore and we got separated in '98." (Halima, first married at 17; widowed at 28; remarried in UK at 36; separated at 41)

Other women, however, had more positive recollections of marriage and the entry to a new family:

"I was lucky. My life there wasn't too different. There was no one to bother me. They accepted me. My in-laws were good, they were happy with me." (Fazira, married at 17)

"It changed a lot. You have a new family so it is different. I didn't have any parent-in-laws, just brother-in-laws and they were all nice to me. I didn't have to do any cooking or anything. There were a lot of people there. They were good to me.... I think whatever parents choose for their children is good. They won't choose anyone bad. It is up to you to cope with it." (Jubera, married at 23)

"I did what they told me to. I helped them with the cooking. I was very young and didn't know how to do anything. I had been studying. I wasn't kept at home, my parents never made me work. At first I couldn't do anything at their house, then I slowly learnt. I had to be very patient, but they were very patient with me too." (Shanaz, married at 14)

"It was good. I was really happy. He was a very good man and loved me very much. We had a lot of love in our life. He was such a good man. He was very fun man. He loved me so much. We never argued – not even one day. He loved me so much and I loved him. He would call me such sweet things.... He was such a loving man. We had a beautiful life together." (Asiya, married at 17)

Whatever the initial experiences of marriage, migration and childbearing would have more crucial long-term influences on the women's lives. At the point of interview, the women had been married for an average of 24.5 years. There was some confirmation in the study for the tendency of early migrants to marry wives younger than themselves. This was most likely due to the fact that by the time that men who had migrated returned to marry, they were older than the typical age of marriage for males in Bangladesh. And since females tended to marry in their mid to late teens, a natural age gap emerged as older brides were not readily available. Eade et al (1996), citing data from Samples of Anonymised Records, note that the average age of Bangladeshi husbands is 10 years older when compared with their wives. Questions about age may, however, be subject to different interpretations, as well as uncertainty about the exact age of husbands and wives. Some illustrations from the study of the latter include:

"My age probably isn't my real age anyway – you know how it is in our country, they always add on a few years to your passport." (Rohima, aged 43)

"My date of birth is 1962. That's my real date of birth, it says 1960 on my passport. I got married at 14, but for this country you have to be 16 to get married, so they lied on my passport for me to come here." (Asma, aged 41)

"I think I may be three or four years younger than my official date of birth. They just wrote that date for my passport. It says 1963 but I think I may have been 19 when I came to this country." (Ruji, aged 37)

"I was actually younger but if they said that then I couldn't have legally got married could I? I don't know how old I really was. There is no account of these things there (in Bangladesh). I was probably about 14. I got married while I was still at school." (Shanaz, aged 52)

To allow for these types of uncertainty, as well as requesting estimates of the husbands' age, respondents were asked whether their husbands were about the same age (five years older or younger), slightly older (up to 10 years), or considerably older (11 years or more) than themselves. Taking only those currently married, 41% reported that their husband was roughly the same age as themselves; 28% said slightly older; and 32% reported that they were considerably older (33% had husbands with an estimated age of 60 and above).

Age differences between husband and wife were also reflected in the wide spread of ages among children in the household (a point illustrated in the case studies of different family types). To a large extent this reflects the way in which family life had one phase in Bangladesh, and another in the UK. The majority of the women had started families in Bangladesh (40% had three or more children before arriving in the UK) and then completed their family in their new home in London. In terms of household structure, this means that most of the women have children aged from under 12 through to those in their twenties and occasionally thirties. For our respondents this often meant responsibility for a wide range of care tasks, from young children to older husbands and relatives. The impact this had on the everyday life of the women in the study is now examined.

Everyday life: rural/urban contrasts

During the interview the women were asked to describe: first, a 'typical' day in their life; second, to think about this day in comparison to the one which they might have had if they were still living in Bangladesh. Taking the former, coding of the replies brought out the centrality of household tasks (mentioned by 83%) and care within the home (76%), followed by religious activities (61%) as a third major strand (leisure-related activities were listed by 28%). Here are accounts from four women about a typical day in their life:

"In the morning I get the children ready for school, dress them, feed them breakfast, then drop them off. Then at home I have my youngest and he needs looking after. I do the cooking and cleaning ... that needs to be done every day. I pray at prayer times. Then I go and pick up the children from school at 3.30. Then at 4.30 I drop them off to Bangla School and pick them up at 6. At 7 they go to Arabic classes and come home at 9. They go to Arabic on Thursday, Friday and Saturday, and Bangla classes Monday to Thursday." (Nuresa, married with four children)

"My whole day goes with my housework." (Waheeda, married with five children)

"I have no time! All this time I am giving you [the interviewer] ... I could have done so much! I could have done the cooking for them. After I come home from dropping them at school, I cook for them. I pick them up from school and after they have eaten, at 4.30 I take them to the mosque. Then I come home and do some more cooking, if it needs to be done. At 7 I bring them home and feed them immediately and sit them down to any homework they have. If they don't have homework, they do reading. Akil needs his daily exercise and then I have to put his special shoes on. Putting those shoes on him, exercising him, this is extra work isn't it? I need to have everything else in order before I can take time to do this." (Rupa, separated, 10 children and caring for two grandchildren)

"I get up in the morning and I pray. Then I wake the children up, get them ready and take them to school. When I come home I cook and watch TV. If I need to I go out and do some shopping. Then I pick up the children from school. When I bring them home it is a bit of a rush to feed them and get them ready for their Arabic classes. They can go all together by themselves, but I pick them up because it gets late." (Nazia, separated, seven children)

Other women reported a wider range of activities running alongside or replacing certain types of care-work:

"I'm doing a course from this September. It's a three months course. It should help me pass my time too when the children are in school and I'm alone in the house." (Saika, married with five children)

"I do a lot of gardening. That passes my time." (Hafiza, divorced, no children)

"Two days a week I go to the gym for exercise and two days a week I go to language classes." (Habiba, married with four children)

"I always feel so hurried. I get really fed up! After I do everything then I get ready for college. I go to ESOL [English for Speakers of Other Languages] classes on Monday and Tuesdays 10-12, then I do IT from 1-3. I do IT five days a week. On Fridays I do Childcare level 3 NVQ. I only do that on Fridays, but I have to do so much for it – it is a lot of hard work! There is so much coursework!" (Asma, married with three children)

"I go to college. I go to Arbour Square three days a week for ESOL classes and two days a week I go to Bethnal Green college and I go on placement one day a week for my childcare course." (Halima, separated, one child)

"I go to my English class three days a week – Monday, Tuesday and Wednesday." (Nazma, widowed, one child)

Caring for school-age children was a major focus of everyday life for the majority of women. However, coping with the ill-health of their husband was also significant for many of those interviewed. Thirty-two per cent of the women reported that they

Mother returning home with children after school

currently provided personal care to someone in the home, the majority of those being partners with chronic health problems:

"He can't do anything for himself. When I go to college I put his meal in the microwave and set the timer so all he has to do is press start. I go at one and come back at three. In that time he prays and eats. He is always in a lot of pain, so I have to spend as much time with him as I can, in case he needs anything. I worry about him all the time." (Rohima, five children)

"We can't do anything together, he is very ill. He has had five heart attacks. He has diabetes, high pressure, skin disease all over his body, and psychiatric problems. Some days he is very ill, other days it's not too bad ... I am just kept busy by him. Give him this, give him that, he wants to eat this, then he doesn't, this is good, then it's not. That takes up my whole day.... They were going to give us a nurse to look after him at home, but he doesn't want that – he can't think properly, and he just says that he doesn't want a nurse, he wants me to do everything. And we just want to do whatever keeps him happy, so we haven't got a nurse." (Salma, six children)

"I have to give him medicine. I have to watch him all night because he could choke. He is fitted to a machine to help him breathe. I can't sleep because I am worried about him and because my sugar levels get high and I get dizzy." (Jannat, four children)

"He has had three operations on his leg. I have to bathe him, get his food ready. Help him dress. He has diabetes and so he needs special food. It is very difficult getting him in and out of the bath. I have heard that people can have bars fitted to help them get into the bath. But we haven't got anything." (Sani, six children)

How did the women compare daily life in Bangladesh with the kind of life that they had now? Following on from the previous discussion, 39% mentioned that they might have had more help around the home if they were in Bangladesh. In some cases these would be members of the women's own family network, but they might in addition be servants (often an unmarried or widowed woman with a child of her own) who would be employed to provide help around the home[3]:

"In Bangladesh it would be easier, there are people around to help, and you have all your family there. If I had one or two of my sisters here, it would be much easier for me. My mother would have shared her time between us." (Toslima, divorced with four children)

"The only good thing is that there would be people available to help with the work. You could bring a woman in. Here you have to do everything yourself." (Sadika, married with six children)

"In Bangladesh it would be different. There are lots of people around. I would have my mother-in-law and sister-in-laws to help. Everyone would be together. Their uncles could take them to school. I wouldn't have to do that duty." (Khadija, married with four children)

"It is much harder in this country. Here we have to take them to school, bring them home, they need so many things. It was never like this in Bangladesh. In Bangladesh I would have more help. In this country I am on my own. I have to do everything. I have been cleaning the house since this morning. Children in this country aren't very good at cleaning are they? So I have to do it all myself." (Rafeya, married with five children)

"In Bangladesh it would be different. I wouldn't have to worry about taking them to school – someone else would do that. I could keep a woman to do all the work for me! In the morning she would bring me a cup of tea and I could just rest all day! It is such a comfortable life there!" (Shumie, married with three children)

"If I was in Bangladesh then it would have been comfortable because I would have had people to help me. What I'm doing now…it's more than I can manage … because there's only one of me in the house looking after six children. My husband is ill and I have to look after him too. It's too much for me. But if I was in Bangladesh, I would have had a helper. I wouldn't have had to work so hard. Everyone wants a bit of rest for themselves." (Feroza, married with six children)

However, at the same time, most of the women did not view returning to Sylhet as an obvious solution to their problems. Indeed, many of the women – at various points in the interview – emphasised the advantages of migration, for themselves as well as their children:

"In Bangladesh it would be very different. There aren't these kind of opportunities are there? Or there might be, but they would only be in the towns, not in the villages. There I would just be at home all day. Here I can go out more." (Alima, married with one child)

"I wouldn't have had all these opportunities, and I would have never known what these opportunities were! But I am glad I am here because I am learning new things, and meeting new people. I meet different people, I have one group of friends in my ESOL classes, and another in my childcare. Last year I registered as a childminder. I think it is good that I have learnt all these things and I can do something for myself now." (Asma, married with three children)

---

[3] The authors are grateful to Kate Gavron for drawing their attention to this point.

"It would have been harder in Bangladesh. There would be more worries. There is more work to do there. In this country you don't have to worry about harvests and crops, in Bangladesh you do. There is a lot of outdoor work. Here it is all indoors." (Sadika, married with six children)

For some respondents, the question of going back has little meaning given the lack of resources in Bangladesh, an aspect that carries particular force for those whose family life has changed with widowhood or separation. Rupa, who was now separated from her husband, comments:

"My life has changed. I am lucky that Allah has looked after me. It could have been worse – what if I was in Bangladesh? I would have nothing. He [husband] wouldn't have fed me or clothed me. At least in this country I am eating, I can wear what I want. I can find the strength to make my children into good people. If I was in Bangladesh I may not have been able to do this much. Who knows what he [her husband] would have done to us. What he would have done to the children. Being in this country I have the power to make my children into good people."

Nazmin, a widow with eight children, addresses the issue simply in terms of survival:

"How would I eat in Bangladesh? At least here I am getting some money from the government. In Bangladesh I would have nothing. This country has good and bad things about living here. No place is perfect."

Finally, a factor influencing many of the responses was the contrast between the overcrowding and physical restrictions of inner-city living, compared with what many viewed as the 'openness' of village life. Thirty-five per cent of the women expressed the advantages of living in Bangladesh in terms of being 'less confined to the home' (see Gardner, 2002, for similar comments from her sample of older women):

"In this country you just sit at home and do everything in the house. You are house-bound. In Bangladesh the village is an open place, you could go and see someone, or walk down to the pond. You get more exercise. You walk around a lot more and get more fresh air. It is better for your health in Bangladesh." (Aklisun, arrived 1985)

"In Bangladesh it would be different. You could go out more, see people. It is an open place, not like here. Here you just have to sit at home. I think my health would have been better there too. It would never be so cold and I would get out more." (Sufia, arrived 1982)

"In Bangladesh you could leave all your doors open. In this country you can't do that. And in Bangladesh you don't have to go out unless you want to. Here you have to go out at least twice to go to the school." (Gulnehar, arrived 1985)

"It would be different in Bangladesh. It's much more open there. You can live differently. You always have fresh air. Here we only go out if we need shopping. Otherwise you shut the door and sit inside." (Sabera, arrived 1991)

These comments must be placed, however, within the context of the pressures arising from the housing conditions of the respondents. They may also reflect the isolation of some of those interviewed – especially within the context of heavy demands in respect of care work and housework – from the company of other women, an issue raised in a study of Mirpuri women in Bradford in the late 1970s (cited in Werbner, 1990). In this context, despite the existence of networks that made migration a realisable goal, some dislocation was inevitable. Social networks were themselves, especially in the economic conditions prevailing when the women arrived in the UK, under strain from the effects of poor housing and deteriorating community relations. These factors certainly contributed to the difficulties facing the women as they confronted the task of caring for people from both older and younger generations.

Conclusion

A key finding from this chapter has been the multiple transitions experienced by migrant women, with various geographical moves as well as changes in social status often compressed into short periods of time. Moreover, such changes often came at critical periods in the life course – such as around the time of marriage or with the birth of children. In Becker's (1997) terms, these were highly disruptive changes involving separation from both an established network of people and daily routines. On the other hand, given the nature of 'chain migration', moves were facilitated and mediated by social networks comprising family and friends; these were crucial in providing support and assistance to the women. Re-establishing contact with relatives already resident in the UK also helped to assist adaptation. Such observation has been reported fairly consistently in studies of transnational migrants. Christine Ho for example, in her research on Afro-Trinidadian networks in Los Angeles comments that:

> ... the chain migration process which participants in this research have used to migrate to the United States is contingent upon the activation of primary social relationships, namely kinship and friendship. Sponsorship by kinsmen in the receiving country is indispensable to potential migrants. Kinsmen are also vital for mediating the actual transfer and initial settlement. Most importantly, kinsmen are fundamental to the adaptation of migrants transplanted to a strange land. They assist in the adaptation process by simultaneously keeping alive long-standing cultural traditions and by providing a foundation from which migrants may be socialized into new and different patterns of behaviour. (1991, p 168)

Gardner also comments on what she sees as the crucial importance for women of extended kin networks and "physical proximity to other Bengali families" (2002, p 128). On the other hand, it might also be said that networks (especially for the women in this study) have clear views about the kind of adaptation that is most appropriate for the new migrant. Women were (as suggested in Chapter One) in many instances brought over to undertake a variety of caring roles – for husbands, children and relatives. In this respect, for these first generation migrants, gender inequalities within Bangladeshi culture were, as Kabeer (2000) argues, largely reproduced within the British context. It is clear also that the strains in the patriarchal contract observed in Bangladesh were also present in Britain, and in many cases magnified due to the limitations of the wider support system. Women were undertaking substantial caring roles, but often with very little direct financial support coming from their husbands. This inevitably brought a significant degree of strain to family relationships; one exacerbated by the pressure of poor housing and problems within the wider community. Both of these were an important backdrop to the everyday lives of the women and the next chapter turns to a more detailed consideration of these elements.

Community and financial resources

Studies of Bangladeshis in Tower Hamlets by Gavron (1997) and Pollen (2002) have both emphasised the difficult accommodation problems facing women arriving in the borough in the 1970s and early 1980s. Lack of affordable, good quality housing was certainly a key issue at that time. A more general issue, however, was the absence of a social policy focusing on the housing needs of large families. Hilary Land's study *Large families in London* had been published in 1969, and had demonstrated the problems facing families with five or more children. Land's research concluded that: "Most of the families [in the study] were unable to obtain accommodation of sufficient size to meet their needs. In London large flats and houses are expensive in the private market and in short supply amongst council dwellings" (1969, p 35). This finding was echoed in an earlier enquiry *Housing in Greater London* (Milner Holland Report), published in 1965. Milner Holland argued that: "The people who suffered most from housing stress are those with the lowest incomes, those with average incomes and large families and many of the newcomers to London" (cited in Land, 1969, p 32).

The arrival of families from Bangladesh in the 1970s was to pose a fresh challenge to the housing market, one reinforced by economic recession and the crisis in public spending that unfolded from the mid-1970s. At the point of interview, our respondents had spent an average of nearly 18 years in the UK (mainly in Tower Hamlets). Given this length of time, first, how had the respondents fared in respect of access to suitable housing? Second, and more generally, what had been their experience of living in an inner-city community? Third, what kind of

financial resources had they accumulated over this period?

Housing histories

The women had been in their present accommodation for an average of 11.4 years. Just over one fifth (22%) had been at the same address for 15 or more years. In the majority of cases, people had moved to their present address from one within Tower Hamlets itself, or for 30% from another inner London borough. This confirms the picture of a group coming directly to the East End in the 1970s and 1980s, making a number of moves within the area before settling in their current home. Mostly these were flats (for 80%), which were rented from the local authority. Six per cent owned their property outright; 13% had a mortgage on the property. How satisfied were the women with their accommodation? Although reported levels of satisfaction (at 68%) were high, those able to cite at least one problem with their accommodation (at 86%) were even higher. The main concerns in respect of housing included: no place to sit outside (identified by 58 women (67%) of those with problems), problems with damp (56 women, 65%), and shortage of space (53 women, 62%). An open-ended question asking people to raise 'any other problems' with their accommodation brought out some of the difficulties facing families with a spread of age groups in cramped living conditions:

"I sleep with my two daughters and a son in another room. Their father sleeps here [in the lounge]. It is becoming a problem. He [the son] is 13 now ... he shouldn't be sharing a room with us. Where would I move this bed too? How can we sleep? Allah has given us all eyes – I can't sleep with my husband in front of my children can I? It is bad enough having a growing boy in the room with two young daughters." (Sufia, married with five children)

"We only have two bedrooms. We sleep with one son and daughter, in our room, and the two older daughters share the other room." (Nuresa, married with four children)

"These children need their own rooms, they shouldn't be sleeping together, boys and girls. If I could speak English then I would ask them, 'You sleep children one to a room. Would you put a 16-year-old girl and a 17-year-old boy in the same room, in the same bed? But you let Bengalis sleep like that'. Now it is warmer I have put some of the children on the floor to sleep. It is too hot for them all in the bed together. I don't know why we are paying rent. I want to stop paying the rent because they don't help." (Fahima, married with three children)

"There are 10 of us in a three-bedroomed house. When they gave us this house they said they would move us within five years. We already had six children by then, but because they were all young it was okay. They said they would transfer us when the children were a bit older. Now the children are older they are saying that we should move our children. One of the bedrooms is very small and two of them are okay. My three daughters sleep in one bedroom and my five sons in another. It is causing too many problems. The children are all grown up and they don't want to be cramped together. They want their own space. The sitting room isn't big enough for us all to sit here." (Gulabi, married with eight children)

Some of the comments underline the desperation and anxiety felt by many of the women:

"See how I am living with my house. There is a degree of shame isn't there with children growing up, how can we sleep in the same room and same bed as our young children?" (Rushna, married with five children)

"There are nine of us in this flat. You can see for yourself how we are living. We have to sleep in the sitting room as well." (Ferdousi, married with seven children)

"We have four grown up children ... the rooms are very small, we can only put single beds in them. We have a bed in the sitting room and they have to sleep on the floor too. They put us in here as temporary housing. We are still waiting to move. They don't let us know anything." (Husna, married with seven children)

Fifty-two per cent of the women were living in a block without access to a lift, which often created problems given their own state of health (see Chapter 5), as well as that of their husbands:

"It is hard because there is no lift in the building. My husband has problems getting up and down the stairs. It is hard for me too. Especially when we have shopping." (Jannat, married with four children)

"There is no lift in this building. My husband is not well and it is difficult for him to climb up to the fifth floor." (Sani, married with six children)

"The lifts don't work and there are always boys having drugs on the stairs. It is very frightening. The main door is supposed to be locked but they break it. They always break the lifts. Me and my husband are both not well and it is difficult for him to climb all these stairs. The lift is always broken." (Mukta, married with seven children)

"There is no lift in the building. The stairs are very hard. My husband had an operation on his veins two months ago so it is hard for him to come up and down the stairs." (Jubera, married with three children)

"We don't have a lift in this building, so we use the lift in the next building and come across to ours. But that lift is never working." (Sabina, married with eight children)

"There is no lift in the building and I have heart problems. It is difficult for me to get up and down the stairs." (Nazifa, married with three children)

Twenty-seven per cent of the women reported that either their own health or that of someone else in the household had been made worse by the state of the

Housing estate – Spitalfields

*Bathroom with rotting window frames,
clothes soaking in buckets*

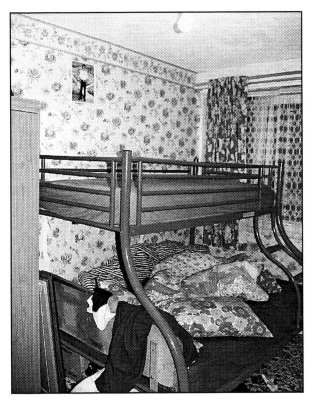

Bedroom space for three children

*Landing area in flat, space used for hanging washing and
drying clothes*

housing. Damp and mould in flats were singled out as major culprits:

"It is very damp. The whole flat smells of damp. We have to re-paper the rooms every year. The council don't do it. I got asthma and hayfever from sleeping in a damp room. The doctor told me to move to a warmer room, so I did. But I have gone back to the damp room now because I have given the other room to my granddaughter. I don't want her to be ill." (Dina, widow with eight children)

"It is very damp and cold here. Two of the rooms are so cold that it is hard for anyone to sleep there. The council have come and seen it and done some work, but it keeps coming back. If anyone stays in the cold rooms they get very ill from the cold." (Amina, widow with six children)

"This house has made us all ill. The whole flat is damp. One of my sons has asthma and one of my daughters is rotting away with eczema. They should have their own rooms and their own beds, not all piled together." (Sufia, married with five children)

Beena, married with five children, brings together the various concerns with housing in the following way:

"One of the rooms is too cold ... no one can sleep there. We told the council, but they don't do anything about it. We have to use fan heaters and that makes the bills come high. The walls are so damp that you can see the water. And we only have one bathroom and toilet in this flat. There are eight of us who live here. It is a problem in the mornings when the children have to go to school."

In the 1960s, Land reported that three quarters of the council tenants in her sample of large families lived in overcrowded conditions (using the Census definition of 1.5 persons per room). Eade et al (1996) reported that the 1991 Census found nearly a fifth (19%) of Bangladeshi households living at over 1.5 persons per room (compared with less than 0.5% of the total resident population and 8% of Pakistani households). Kempson's (1999) research found 43% of Bangladeshis living in households with insufficient bedroom space (compared with 3% of all households).

The families in this study were living at an average of 1.518 persons per room. Fifty-six per cent were living at a density of 1.5 or more persons per room, while 27 of the families were living two or more to a room. These figures suggest that the crisis in housing large families, described by Hilary Land some 40 years previously, has hardly lessened in the intervening period. For some families there seemed little prospect of any immediate improvement. Sufia arrived in Tower Hamlets in 1982 and is married with five children. She lives in a two-bedroom flat and comments that:

"We applied for a bigger flat in 1982, and we are still waiting."

Fahima, who arrived in the area in 1985, and is living in a three-bedroom flat with her husband and nine children, describes her situation as follows:

"They put me on the transfer list as soon as I moved in here. They said that I would get a house within six months. It has been 15 years now. They won't give me a house. If I go to the council they say that there are other people on the waiting list and I have to wait my turn. They say I have to get 1,000 points. How am I supposed to get 1,000 points? We are on 295 points. I have nine children – what do I have to do to get more points?"

Other women had similar stories:

"We have been on the waiting list since 1985 and the council won't re-house us." (Zaima, married with seven children, living in a three-bedroom flat for 19 years)

"We have been on the waiting list for 12 years now. If we go to them they say that we don't have enough points. How are we supposed to raise our points? They gave us this flat when we had two children, now I have had three more children. They say we don't have enough points, or they don't have any houses." (Rushna, married with five children, living in a two-bedroom flat for 12 years)

"We have been on the waiting list for 16 years. They have just offered us a flat. We went to see it but it is not very nice. But I am worried that if we refuse it they may keep us waiting another 16 years before they offer us another one." (Mala, married with five children, living in a three-bedroom flat for 17 years)

Gardner (2002, p 132) makes the point that the relationship between physical space and gender roles is a circular one: on the one hand, flats are likely to be too small for most nuclear families, let alone extended kin. On the other hand, this means that women (especially with young children) often have less support than they might have had in Bangladesh (a common complaint from our respondents). The result is both a reinforcement of traditional gender roles and, for some, a significant degree of isolation within the local community.

Neighbourhood life

Housing was, therefore, a major concern for the respondents. However, to what extent was this mitigated by a favourable experience of the community itself? The women in the study were drawn from a range of areas within Tower Hamlets, including Stepney, Bow, Whitechapel, Wapping and Poplar. They had lived in their neighbourhoods for an average of 12 years. What kind of social contacts and relationships did the women have within the community? Given the concentration of Bangladeshis in Tower Hamlets, it is perhaps not surprising that close to two thirds of the women (60%) could name a relative such as a sister, cousin or a niece within the borough. Neighbourhood relationships in this context overlapped with kinship ties – a continuation of a long-standing tradition in the East End as reported by Ellen Ross (1983) and Young and Willmott (1957) among others.

Eighty-nine per cent of the women had friends in their neighbourhood, with the majority reporting that they spoke to them either daily or two or three times a week. Most of these friends were drawn from within the Bangladeshi community, however, 17% reported having friends from a variety of ethnic groups. These had been formed through contacts at school, work, education classes and through their own children:

"I have all kinds of friends – English, Caribbean, Pakistani. One of my best friends is Caribbean and I have known her since I was at school. Most of my non-Bengali friends I know from school or college

days or I meet them through work." (Fazila, Bethnal Green)

"They [her friends] have been my friends for a long time. They are my son's friends' mothers. One is African and there are Pakistani women too. And I have some good English friends from my classes." (Alima, Wapping)

"I have two English friends and one Jamaican. They come to see me and I go to their houses too. One of them works in a bank and her husband works in the council. The English ones were my classmates when I did my child care course in 1995. I met them then. We exchanged [telephone] numbers in class and now we are good friends and visit each other often." (Asma, Stepney)

These comments illustrate the way in which social networks can be broadened through involvement in different activities within the community, an aspect that is discussed in more detail in Chapter 6. However, they are also dependent on evaluations of the locality in which people reside – whether it is safe, whether people feel secure inside and outside their homes, whether people feel free from racist attacks. In many respects, the women were very positive about living in their neighbourhood. Virtually all of the respondents (91%) identified something that they liked about their immediate locality, with access to amenities such as a mosque, doctors, food shops and transport, being the key elements:

"The outside of the building is nice and open and the children can play outside safely. It is a safe area. The transport is good – the buses and underground. And the mosque is near." (Fazira, Bethnal Green)

"The shops are quite close and it's a nice quiet area." (Jannat, Wapping)

"The area is good. Everything is close by. The buses are good and we have the trains and the doctor close too." (Sabera, Poplar)

"The shops and school are close by. The buses and trains are all good here. It is a good area to live in." (Lutfa, Poplar)

Grocer's shop on Brick Lane

Shuara, however, expressed a contrary view:

"There are lots of Bengali people here [in Shoreditch], and that is good for us. You [to interviewer] can speak English and so you would be alright in an area with English people. I can't speak English, so if I go out and I see a Bengali person, then I know that I can speak to them if I want to. That is good. This is a good Bengali place – you might as well call it Sylhet! This is our own Sylhet."

Only a minority of the women (42%) could think of anything to dislike about their neighbourhood; the major concern being the various social problems that were seen as affecting the area. Interestingly, for at least some of the women, this was attributed to being surrounded by too many Bangladeshi neighbours:

"All the English people near us are very nice. Since we have been here, we have never had any problems. Instead, now it's the Bengali boys who are pestering us! They congregate downstairs and just cause problems! But the English are fine...They have never troubled us." (Saleha, Whitechapel)

"There are too many Bengali people. When we first came there was mainly English people here and it was very comfortable living here, and it was much cleaner. There was much less trouble and fighting. Now it's awful. There is a lot of fighting. There are some very bad gangs around here." (Khayrun, Whitechapel)

"There's too many Bangladeshis. There's too many fights among them. Any area where there's too many of our people is where there's too much fights and things." (Saika, Shadwell)

"I used to really like this area, but now they've ruined it by crowding it with lots of bad people ... really bad people. Before I was so comfortable here. They're our people but the bad type." (Makhan, Bow)

On the other hand, some women, although stressing that they had good neighbours, also expressed frustration at being unable to communicate with them. Shuara, who has been in the UK for around 10 years, commented that:

Brick Lane shop window

"I can't speak any other language so how would I make friends? They [neighbours] are nice to me and say 'hello' and other things. But I don't understand what they are saying. They do try and talk, but I don't understand what they are saying. The English and Jamaicans in this area are very nice. There is a Jamaican woman downstairs and she adores my grandson. She always stops to talk with him [but] I don't have a clue what she is saying!"

Worries and concerns about the area were often linked to drug-related problems and disputes between gangs:

"The area has become very bad. You can't go out in the evenings, they are on the stairs, and they stop the lift and use that for their drugs and they are sick in the lift, and they leave behind the things they use for their drugs. This is becoming a big problem for our children." (Aklisun, Whitechapel)

"This isn't a good area to bring up children. There is a lot of trouble, you must have heard about the reputation of this area? There is a lot of drug-taking, shouting, fighting. They have set fire to the lift many times. But what can you do? Where can we go?" (Neefa, Wapping)

"There are always boys having drugs on the stairs. It is very frightening." (Mukta, Poplar)

"I don't like it because it's our own people and our own children who are fighting in gangs. Boys hang around in the area 24 hours a day ... 16-year-olds ... 15-year-olds ... 18-year-olds.... They spit at girls who pass and tease them and push them.... And you see them taking drugs ... smoking cigarettes ... downstairs near our stairs ... I have complained so much ... there's nothing I can do ... I want to move away from here but we need money to go away and buy a bigger house." (Saika, Shadwell)

"Recently I have become concerned about the young boys in the area. I am a bit scared of going out. I haven't had any trouble directly, but I am a bit worried. They don't respect their elders anymore. Now these children are shouting and just very rude. My house has been burgled three times and our car has been broken into twice and they have stolen my disability badge. It is really expensive fixing the window – just last week it happened again, the car is still in the garage so it makes it very difficult for me to get about." (Jusna, Bethnal Green)

Taylor argues that drug problems among Bangladeshi youth date back at least to the early 1990s, and that overcrowded living conditions have made them especially vulnerable. He comments:

Bangladeshi youth [spend] a lot of time on the street and [are] more likely, therefore to come into contact with both pushers and abusers. Youth workers [report] that children as young as eleven [are] already addicted.... In 1998 a third of the young drug-users attending the Community Drugs Team facilities would be Bangladeshi boys, often brought along by their concerned sisters. (2001, p 281)

Table 4.1 summarises the results from four statements dealing with different aspects of personal safety within the community. This shows 39% of the women as feeling 'very or fairly worried' about being mugged or robbed, and 31% as 'very or fairly worried' about being physically attacked because of their colour. On two related questions, virtually all of the women (96%) felt safe in their own homes at night, compared with 67% who said that they would feel unsafe if out alone in the neighbourhood after dark. Some of the women spoke openly about problems of racism, an issue explored in a range of sociological studies covering the East End (Phillipson et al, 2001). Neefa, who lives in Wapping, recalls an incident from some years ago that has stayed in her mind:

"My husband got beaten up by racists. Skinheads beat him up and he needed stitches on both sides of his head. This was many years ago, just after my eldest son was born. In those days there weren't many Bengalis in this area. It was in the summertime and he was coming home. It was about nine o'clock ... it was still light ... the days were long. And he came to get into the lift. As he got in, they got in with him and started hitting him. He fainted. After that I was very scared and didn't go out for a long time."

Farida and her family in Poplar had a number of bad experiences with their neighbours and they decided to take an extended stay in Bangladesh to get away from some of their problems:

Table 4.1: Worries about personal safety (%)

	Very worried	Fairly worried	Not very worried	Not at all worried
Having your home broken into	7	21	38	34
Being mugged or robbed	12	27	30	31
Being physically attacked because of your colour	11	20	32	37
Being physically attacked because of your ethnic origin or religion	10	20	33	37

N = 100

"They were English and they gave us a lot of trouble. They would always shout and argue with us and one day they came round with a knife. We had three young children and I didn't want to stay there. We were very scared so we went back [to Bangladesh]. We came back after they gave us another house."

Husna, living in Poplar, has continuing experiences of racism on the streets:

"It is very racist here. My husband was abused yesterday. They called him 'Osama'. I am too scared to go out. I don't let my children go out either. We would like to move out of the area. It has been like this in this area. They take my husband's prayer cap off his head. Once they took it off his head and urinated in it. The English boys go around in big groups. It is very frightening."

Nurun, also living in Poplar, talked about the intimidation encountered on the streets:

"We have a big racial problem too. We can't go out of the house. Even when I take my children to school the English women are so abusive. They will stand in my way and not let me pass. Yesterday after dropping off the children [at school] I was walking back with a friend and this woman came towards us and she had three dogs with her. One of them was huge, and she came and was pushing her dogs onto us. The more I tried to move away the more she pushed her dogs towards me."

The same respondent also talked about some of the problems she had at her children's school, even to the extent of feeling vulnerable to abuse from other mothers when picking up her children:

"I am too scared to take my mother-in-law with me. She could do with the walk ... but after school when the children come out ... the children and the mothers just push you. They try to push you over. This is a very racist area. When I bring my children home I come the long way round. It is too bad trying to come the short way. My children have a racism problem too. They are always being picked on at school."

Financial resources

Problems with housing, along with experiences of racism within the community, were reinforced by the financial pressures facing the women. This aspect may be seen as of crucial importance in promoting the quality of life for a group of women with substantial domestic responsibilities. What did the interviews reveal on this issue? Table 4.2 sets out the main benefits received by the respondents. The reliance on means-tested benefits, such as Income Support (65%) and housing and related benefits (66%), is an important finding. Other sources of income included: Child Benefit (86%), Council Tax Benefit (59%) and Severe Disablement Allowance (20%). The women were asked to give an estimate of their weekly household income, taking all sources into consideration (that is, benefits, interest on savings, maintenance). Seventy were able to provide information, producing a mean income of £183.31; 21 (30%) had incomes below £150. One third of the women reported that one or more of their children made a financial contribution to the running of the home, and in the majority of cases this was done on a regular basis (weekly or monthly).

In terms of paid work, only two women were currently in employment, with a further two describing themselves as unemployed. Ninety-one per cent of the women defined themselves as 'looking

Table 4.2: Access to benefits

	% In receipt
Child Benefit	86
Rent Rebate/ Rent Allowance	66
Income Support	65
Council Tax Benefit	59
Severe Disablement Allowance	20
Working Families' Tax Credit	15
Disability Living/Mobility/Attendance Allowance	14
National Insurance Retirement Pension	12
Jobseeker's Allowance	11
Invalid Care Allowance	3

after the family, home or dependants'. Only a minority of the women currently not working had ever been in any kind of paid employment. However, an important finding from this study is that of the 81 women who provided information, 38 (47%) said that they would have liked paid work outside the home. Among this group of 81 women, the main obstacles to securing employment were seen in terms of pressures associated with caring for young children (31 women), lack of fluency in English (23), and no desire to work (15).

Responsibilities for children were key issues for many of the women, limiting the feasibility of employment beyond the home:

"If I didn't have any children after I came to this country, then I would have worked. I don't like living like this. I would prefer to work and get money. If you go out to work your body stays healthy." (Ranu, married with five children)

"I never even got the chance so what's the point of wanting? Obviously I would have wanted to work. Who doesn't want to hold their own money? But my children were young and I had to look after them." (Rafeya, married with five children)

"I want to do childminding and do the course for it. But it's difficult to do anything else because I'm alone with the children. But childminding would have been alright so that I would look after my own children and do the childminding too. I'm doing a course from this September. It's a three months course. I would be able to pass my time too when the children are in

school and I'm alone in the house." (Saika, married with five children)

The desire for work was especially strong among those separated and widowed. At the same time, the comments also suggest the difficulties the women have in getting back into networks that can identify employment opportunities within the community. Fultara, for example, who had been separated from her husband for 12 months, would clearly like to extend the teaching she has undertaken in a voluntary capacity:

"Once I did teach young children Bengali, but that was just for a few weeks before I went to Bangladesh, and then when I came back, I couldn't find that kind of work again. It was just teaching a few children in the building, some of the mothers asked me to do it. When I first came to this country I was better than the men here. All the men in the building would get me to write their letters for them. There were three other Bengali families and two of them would regularly come to me to write their letters for them. And they asked me to teach their children, so I taught both Bengali and Arabic. Now I wish I could find that kind of work, but there isn't any. There are schools all around. If I could find that kind of work I would do it, it would pass away a couple of hours wouldn't it?"

Rukshana, whose husband died 14 years ago, is also anxious to find work but lacks confidence and worries about not speaking English:

"I would like a job if I could get one. The DSS are chasing me to get into work. They want me to go to work. For the last two years they have been telling me to work. Since I stopped getting Child Benefit for my son they have told me to work. That's not a problem, I have to live by the rules of this country. I have said 'fine, give me a job – I have to get by, I need to live' but how can I work? I am so ill I can't even work. But I do want to work, I will do whatever I can. But I can't speak the language, I have never worked, where would I get a job? Who do I ask? But I have gone and looked for a job. I have asked in sari shops but they laugh at me. They say 'we have young girls asking for jobs, why should we give it to an old person like you?' If no one will give me a job what can I do? But I am looking the only way I know how ... I ask people wherever I can. I would rather stand on my own two feet than bother the DSS. But what can I do if no one will give me a job?"

In contrast, Poroush, who had been widowed since 1990, had been able to find a mixture of paid and unpaid work:

"My days are good. I go to work. I think if you sit at home all day then you worry about things. It is not good for you. I go out and work and I see my friends and they are really nice. We get on very well. I work seven days a week. In the week I do cleaning jobs at three different places and on Saturdays I teach at a Bengali school and on Sundays I do outreach work."

And Nazma had become heavily involved in voluntary work since her husband's death:

"I do three days voluntary work at the centre. I help ill people – people who are handicapped, paralysed and disabled. They are all good people – some have mental problems. All kinds of people. There is a special centre...it's a community centre. So I go three days a week, I am a 'caring something', I don't know what they call it."

National surveys have confirmed the low rates of economic activity among Bangladeshi men, in contrast with Black Caribbean and Indian men (PIU, 2001). In this study, there were 75 women currently living with their partners, only 18 (24%) of whom were in paid employment. In terms of the types of jobs of those ever employed, the main ones were tailoring, working in restaurants and factory work. Many of the men had left these jobs at a relatively young age. Taking those partners not in employment, the mean age at which they had left work was 46.47 years. This finding confirms Gavron's (1997) argument that the arrival of spouses in the 1970s and 1980s, along with declining job opportunities and the poor health of many of the men, prompted withdrawal from the labour market. She also comments that:

Men who were already having to adjust themselves to living with their small children in cramped housing had a further adjustment to make: they had to work out a domestic division of labour in these new circumstances. It is hardly surprising that some men chose to live on state benefits and participate in the reproduction of the household rather than continue

to fight for sparse and badly paid local employment. (Gavron, 1997, p 150)

The downside of this strategy was that it exacerbated financial problems within the home. Of the 97 families who answered a question about how they were managing financially, 41 (42%) reported that they were 'just about getting by'; 17 (18%) reported worries about bills; and 16 (17%) stressed the importance of financial help from their family (children especially). Only 22% of the women reported having any 'spare cash' to spend on themselves. Even more revealing, only 20% of the women reported having access to cash in an emergency. A number of comments revealed the difficulties and dilemmas that faced the women in the study. Fahima, married with nine children, comments:

"Before when my husband worked I could afford to want things for myself. Now, do I give my children what they want or do I spend on myself? I would rather give it to my children."

Asma, who has three children, makes a similar point:

"Sometimes I take some bread from home for lunch. I deliberately don't take money for myself, because it has to come from somewhere doesn't it? The money is for my children."

A number of the women mentioned the additional expenses that had to be met for religious teaching for their children:

"In this country you have to pay for religious teaching. The government doesn't pay towards that. We have to pay for ourselves. I have gone without so that we could teach the children about their faith." (Gulabi, married with eight children)

"But it is hard for Bengali and Arabic. We have educated them as much as we can. I taught them as much as I could and now we have to pay a teacher to come and teach them. They charge so much." (Rafeya, married with five children)

"The children need a lot of money. Two of them are at Madrasas that costs us a lot of money. We take money out of the food budget to pay for that." (Husna, married with seven children)

The kinship network was, however, viewed as an importance source for acquiring financial support when needed. The following are examples of how this network operates:

"We had to borrow the money [to pay for our house]. My brothers are very well-off. One of my brothers gave us £10,000. My sons will have to pay him back when they grow up. Other relatives helped us as well." (Rohima, married with five children)

"When we get very big bills we have to borrow the money. So we get £10 from one person and £20 from another and pay them back when we can or if we can." (Jannat, married with four children)

"When we fall short we borrow some money from our neighbours. If we fall short by £10 or £20 he [her husband] borrows." (Kulsuma, married with six children)

"My daughter had to pay for her own wedding and one of my brother-in-laws helped and we are still paying him back slowly." (Fatima, married with nine children)

As already noted, children were probably the main source of help, both for emergency and other needs:

"Sometimes I fall short and then my daughter helps out with £10. When I went on Hajj my son and eldest daughter gave me the money. I went to Bangladesh twice and once my daughter paid, and before that when I went with their father the eldest daughter and our son paid." (Shuara, married with three children)

"Our children help sometimes. When the bills come and we are short they might give us £20 or £30." (Aklisun, married with eight children)

"My two eldest sons live away and they come and see me and help me out." (Shanaz, widow with nine children)

"If the benefit money falls short then my daughters help me out." (Nazmin, widow with eight children)

"My sons help out, they do the shopping." (Dina, widow with eight children)

"When I can't manage I tell my sons and they help me." (Amina, widow with six children)

"I have to borrow money from my daughters sometimes." (Jolikha, widow with four children)

To assess further the extent of deprivation in the sample of women, an index of deprivation was constructed based on seven items illustrating various dimensions of poverty. This comprised:

- Lives in a household with more than one person per room.
- Lives in a household where the head of the household receives Income Support.
- Limited educational attainment.
- Lives in local authority or housing association rented accommodation.
- Respondent has no cash to spend on herself.
- Respondent does not have access to any money in an emergency.
- Respondent does not receive at least one of six types of regular payments (earnings from employment; pension from previous employer; private pension/annuity; income and dividends from shares and investments; income from other sources such as rent or savings; and other kinds of regular allowances outside the home).

The scoring on this measure (with one point given for each item) was: zero for no deprivation; 1–2 low deprivation; 3–4 medium deprivation; and 5 or more indicating high deprivation. The result confirms the very high level of deprivation among the women, with 77% scoring 5 or more; 18% 3–4; and just 5% 2 or below. Even allowing for help from children or relatives (which could set up pressures in the form of loans coming from within the kin network), this was a group under considerable financial strain, as conveyed in some of the following comments:

"I am living off the benefits I get. I will go without to pay the bills. I don't eat so that I can pay the bills. If I can't pay the bill in one go I will pay it in three." (Mariam, widow with five children)

"Nowadays we don't have enough to feed ourselves but we have to buy them toys. We go without food so that the children can have what they want." (Ranu, married with five children)

"Financially it is very hard. The benefit money we get isn't enough. How can we get by with so many children only on our benefits. We don't have anyone working in our family. We have to pay our bills in two or three instalments." (Beena, married with five children)

Conclusion

Despite the supportive networks established by the women, these were clearly placed under considerable strain by overcrowding at home, racism within the wider community, and the financial pressures arising from lack of paid employment[1]. Social networks become vital in supporting the women in this context but the pressures were clearly substantial for many of those interviewed. In some respects, this reflected a running together of social and economic problems. The women were struggling with immense responsibilities for care and support on the one side, but constant pressure from inadequate housing and reliance on Income Support from the state on the other. These difficulties were compounded by the ambiguous social position of first generation migrants – caught as they were between two contrasting cultures. This point is captured precisely by Peggy Levitt in her study of Dominican migrants to Boston (USA), where she observes that:

They watch the Anglo world from its margins, not knowing how to negotiate their way in. They feel more capable when they compare themselves to those who remain [in their home village] and diminished when it comes to dealing in the larger world. Those who regret their choices find it difficult to turn back because so many family members and friends depend on their support. (2001, p 200)

However, transnational ties continued to exert a strong pull for the women in this research. Obligations to care for husbands and children were certainly of major importance, but links with family and friends also had a considerable influence – in some cases creating additional responsibilities. The next chapter examines these ties in more detail, assessing at the same time some of the costs and benefits that migration had brought to the women's lives.

---

[1] The last two may of course be interrelated. Kabeer (2000) reported in her study that Bangladeshi women in the East End cited experiences or fear of racist abuse as reasons to work at home.

Transnational migration: costs and benefits

5

This chapter reviews some of the gains and losses associated with migration from Bangladesh. At the time of interview, the women in the study had been in the UK for approaching 18 years. How did they view the way their lives had developed over this time? In line with the objectives of this research, this chapter focuses on three areas: first, changes in personal and social aspects of identity; second, opportunities and constraints in everyday life; third, transnational connections. A major concern will be with exploring, for each of these areas, how the roles and responsibilities of the women have changed as a consequence of migration.

The possibility of change is a common theme in migration literature. A respondent in Peggy Levitt's study *The transnational villagers* comments: "The woman that migrates develops in many ways. She has to learn how to live alone, to do everything, and not to ask for anything" (2001, p 102). Levitt concludes her study with the view that: "Transnational migration opens up opportunities for some and constitutes a deal with the devil for others" (p 200). Against this, the women in this study certainly had powerful networks in assisting the passage from one country to another. In Werbner's terms (2002, p 6), our respondents were able to "sustain their home culture away from home", thus helping to shield themselves in some way from the world they entered through migration. Yet it is also the case that maintaining links across cultures could itself create pressures, especially for a group with limited economic resources and major responsibilities within the household. This chapter considers how these elements influenced the daily lives of the women in this study.

Religion and identity

Given the length of time that the women had been in the UK, we were interested in assessing how they viewed themselves in relation to key areas of culture and religion. A consistent theme in the literature on transnational communities is the way in which members can develop fluid, often conflicting identities (Levitt, 2001). Gardner, in her work on Bengali elders in Tower Hamlets, makes this point:

> ... people shift their positions according to particular contexts. In some situations they may fix their identities as 'Bangladeshi' or 'Muslim', appearing to adhere to a pre-given set of traditions and essentialized cultural norms, while in others they identify themselves as something more hybrid or complex. This is certainly the case for many of the Bengali elders we spoke to, whose positionality has changed over the life course and within specific contexts during the same period. We should not infer from this that such shifts in position are necessarily conscious, however, or that they are always freely made. Whilst the elders choose their identities and cultural positions, they also, at the same time, have identities and 'cultures' foisted upon them. (2002, p 11)

To examine this issue the women were first asked to provide a description of themselves, with Bengali, Muslim, Sylheti and British presented as the main options. Seventy-nine per cent mentioned being Muslim in their description of themselves. Rushna, for example, comments:

"Our religion is the most important thing for us. There are lots of Bengalis. They can be Hindu or Muslim. That's why we have to say Muslim."

Many of the women emphasised the importance of their faith in providing meaning and direction to their life:

"Islam is the basis for everything. Everything comes back to that. Allah put us on this earth as Muslims. We have to remember that all the time and follow the teachings of the prophet. Allah takes us through each day. I have taught my children Arabic at home myself. It is important that they learn." (Hajera)

"Of course it is important. We have to live according to our faith. That's why I send my children to Arabic classes ... they have a lot of homework to do but I still send them. They need to learn about our faith. What is there without faith?" (Rohima)

"Allah has made us Muslims and we have to follow that. My faith is the most important thing. It gives me peace and removes all my pain. When you pray you move away from everything that is in this world and become closer to Allah." (Monwara)

Two thirds of the women mentioned viewing themselves as Bengali, emphasising different links between culture and religion. Shebin comments that:

"They are both the same. I am Bengali because of where I was born, and Muslim because of who I was born to."

While Shuara sees the balance as:

"The most important is Muslim. Bengali is just our language and our ways of doing things. If I don't pray and fast what good will Bengali do me?"

Some of the women mentioned the process of change and adaptation that migration required in their lives:

It [religion] is important. But I am not over-religious or under-religious. I am just normal. We have to adapt all the time. I don't think it's good to overdo things. We should just be normal. There are people who say that my daughters should wear burkhas and do this or that. But I feel that we have to get on in this country and so we should do things normally. Not overdo things. I think that as long as I teach my children to pray five times a day ... teach them the Quran then they do as much as they want. When they feel the need they can read the Quran. It's no good if I force them to do it and they don't want to. If they manage to pray five times a day then that is good. If they can't then they can make the time if they want to. I have taught them how to do it. That is my duty. The rest is up to them." (Zaima)

Zaima goes on to express the link between different identities:

"They [being Muslim, Bengali, Sylheti] are all equal to me. They are all important to me but as we are in this country and we will stay here then we have to be all three. My children can't tell me anything about Bangladesh ... so I cannot just hold onto the Bengali. As we are in this country we have to live by the customs of this country. If I need to go to the doctor I have to be able to make him understand me and be able to understand him."

Migration, however, had brought other pressures and dilemmas for the respondents; the loosening of norms associated with purdah being one example (see also, Kabeer, 2000):

"Your faith is everything. We have to live by our faith as long as we are in this world. As long as we are living. You have to do as much as you can. It's very hard to do everything that Islam asks us to do. I do as much as I can. Imagine ... in this country I have to go shopping ... so I have to go out. Our religion says that we shouldn't go out too much, and when we do, we should be properly in purdah. But I don't always do it properly. I go to the banks and to the shops. I am aware of what I am doing ... how much I am doing." (Saleha)

"In this country I spend my time watching television, however much I might observe purdah, there is still a purdah of the mind isn't there? It's not possible to have that purdah here. When you put on the television everyone will sit and watch it. The television shows everything. There is no shame in this country." (Leema)

Twenty-eight per cent of the women mentioned seeing themselves as Sylheti, whereas none of those interviewed identified themselves as being British. Asked to say what was the most important of all the different ways of describing themselves, two thirds (66%) mentioned being a Muslim. Asked about the role of faith in her life, Shuara comments:

"It is the most important thing to me. It is all I will take with me when I die. I pray that Allah will take my faith with me when he takes me. That I can die with his name on my lips."

The various comments cited previously have parallels as well as contrasts with second generation Bangladeshis. Eade's (1997b) interviews with young Bangladeshis (also in Tower Hamlets) demonstrated the continuing importance of Muslim, Bangladeshi and Sylheti identities. However, he finds these open to more 'versatile interpretations' than appeared to be the case among the women interviewed in this study. Moreover, in marked contrast, younger Bangladeshis were more likely to embrace the term 'British', invariably separating this out from being 'English'. One of Eade's respondents comments:

I'm British and a Londoner … I don't know why, I just feel to be British you don't actually have to be white. But to be English I always have this feeling you have to be white. British people are not necessarily English … but to be English you have to be white. The English, I think, would agree although they probably wouldn't say directly. (1997b, p 157)

To examine some of these issues, changes between generations were discussed with focus groups comprising younger women at different settings within Tower Hamlets (a group of sixth formers; a group of recent graduates; and a group currently working in various jobs within the borough). The discussion with sixth formers confirmed Eade's point about the mix of identities negotiated by younger Bangladeshis:

Interviewer:	How do you see yourselves in terms of identity?
Silma:	A mix of Muslim, Asian and British.
Nusrat:	British-Asian-Muslim.
Silma:	I'd say Muslim-British-Bengali. I'd like to put the Muslim first because most of my [views] come from Islamic stuff.

Sabia:	Muslim takes priority because my morals and my beliefs come from my religion.
Farhana:	We're Muslims in practice even if we don't wear the scarf. Hopefully we will get to that soon.
Rahmin:	Even though we're British we would all like to be known by our Bengali identity.
Farhana:	Definitely.
Nusrat:	A few years ago I never saw myself wearing a scarf. I don't wear it properly but a few years ago I never saw myself doing that ... and two years ago I never saw myself going to the mosque and wearing it properly and going to the mosque for prayers. But it's progressing and I do want to see myself wearing it properly.
Nadia:	I only recently started wearing a scarf. I never thought I'd be wearing a hijab properly and doing all my prayers.
Silma:	I don't see myself wearing a hijab, but I do my prayers.
Nusrat:	My life goes topsy-turvy if I don't do my prayers.
Silma:	I plan my revision around my prayers! I use my prayers as breaks between topics!

The graduates, aged between 21-23, all emphasised the way in which being a Muslim continued to shape their identity:

Interviewer:	How would you identify yourselves?
Seema:	For me it would definitely be Muslim first. A Bengali Muslim I would say, because I think in terms of my way of thinking it's a lot to do with Islamic values. I wouldn't say 100% Bengali, but there is Bengali in it as well, which I would still teach my children I suppose.
Samina:	When you go to uni your behaviour is more dictated by your religious beliefs than your cultural beliefs. When I'm at uni I don't drink ... I don't eat haram foods, things like that. More people know me as a Muslim, they don't know that I'm a Bengali or anything like that.
Eva:	Definitely the Muslim is first and the most important.
Layla:	Muslim.

Eva, a 22-year-old history graduate, was able to identify with being British, but at the same time also felt somewhat detached:

"The British will always be there because we were born here and brought up here. It would be too long to add British as well! I hate categorising myself. I would never do it. If I had to I would say, yeah, Bangladeshi Muslim, but the thing about British is, although I was born and brought up here, I still feel isolated sometimes. You don't think you fit in, because I don't like some of the things that go on around here, but at the same time there are things that I don't like that go on back home, anyway. So where do I go? But this is ultimately home."

In response to a question about how far people consciously think about identity, Seema suggests that this can sometimes happen when you go into new social contexts:

"Its funny, when I was younger, I used to go to a youth club. We used to go on trips and camping. And every time we went on a trip I used to become more Bengali. We'd go to Scotland and Yorkshire, and every time we went I would pray all the time, at home I didn't used to pray, but when I was out of Tower Hamlets I used to pray, everything. There were other people who would rebel when they were out of Tower Hamlets, but I used to be more Bengali and more Muslim when I was out of the house than when I was at home!"

More generally, there was a sense of being part of a wider Asian community that influenced behaviour and attitudes in a variety of ways:

Seema:	There is a lot we share with the wider Asian community, like the language, you can just chat to them.
Samina:	I think there's loads, like religion and culture.
Eva:	And the food ... we all love our food!
Layla:	Things that we all do. Like we all drag the whole of our families to the airport if just one person is going away.
Layla:	Weddings.
Eva:	The clothes, the food, the family values.
Seema:	Even our marriages. You can talk to your Asian friends about marriage proposals.

Identity remains a complex area for these younger people, and perhaps even more so for the women in our study. However, the dilemmas and uncertainties are reinforced by how individuals experience their immediate environment. To examine this a general concern of this study is now explored: namely how did roles and responsibilities change as a consequence of migration? What were the benefits and costs experienced by the women?

Opportunities and benefits

Faith and religion, it would seem, provided some degree of continuity for the women in this research. At the same time, much had changed for them since coming to Britain. For some, there were feelings of pride and achievement about the direction that their lives had taken over the years. Salma, who had been in the UK for 21 years, echoes the comments of Peggy Levitt's (2001) respondent described at the beginning of this chapter:

"How can you not change coming to a different country? You [to the interviewer] were born in this country. Why don't you go and live in Bangladesh for a few years? Wouldn't you become braver and more confident that you went and lived in another country ... that you coped? You have to have that courage ... that you have come to a new country, you don't have anyone here, so you have to be everything for yourself. You have to get on with things."

A number of women mentioned the first steps they were taking down the road of education classes:

"I went back to living on my own and then I went on to do my B.Ed – teacher training. I had done my BA before getting married, but I didn't work while I was married. After my divorce I did my training, and then went on to teach in primary schools." (Hafiza)

"I have done ESOL classes and am doing a childcare course. I wanted to join the childcare course two years ago but they said my English wasn't good enough so I took the ESOL classes and now they have accepted me." (Halima)

"I am going to English classes. I had an exam recently and I had a good result. But for the speaking part she said I spoke too fast, but that that didn't matter and that would get better. I had to say a story – explain the meaning from pictures on a card. And then she [the teacher] asked me lots of questions as well." (Ruji)

Rupa mentions the benefits she gains from her children's education:

"My children bring books home for me! They say 'Mum, you can read this book – its easy!' and they bring Bengali books too. My grandson Asif, gets books from his school, he says to his teachers 'Give me a book for my grandmother' and then he comes home and says 'Nani, I got you this book from my teacher' so I read them. I read children's books! I am learning from my children! Abid brings home books and says 'Mum, I got you this, its in big letters so it will be easy for you to read'. And my daughter Leena writes things down and tells me to copy her writing! It's good fun. They teach me."

Other women mentioned just having more freedom in their life:

"When I was in Bangladesh I wouldn't go out to do the shopping. Here I have to do that. There isn't anyone to tell me that I can't. I can do what I want." (Jamela)

"In this country you have to go out. If I suddenly need something I will go and get it. In this country you don't have to send anyone to send out to get it for you. I am doing those things now." (Zeba)

Many of the women linked migration with benefits for their children, daughters especially:

"They can study as much as they want to. They can work. Their life has more meaning and use here. In our country they see women as useless, not here. They have more worth here. It is better for them in every way here." (Zaima)

"It is better for studying here. In our country girls can't work or study very much. Here you can study and work, everything is convenient." (Rushna)

"My daughters like it in this country – this is where they were born and brought up. They are used to the way of life here. They don't like Bangladesh and don't want to go there. Everything in this country is

suitable for them – they can study and work and have more freedom here." (Nazia)

These adjustments were reflected in changing practices in areas such as marriage, work and relationships beyond the home. In contrast with their own experience of marriage, of the 46 women with at least one married child, 24 (52%) reported that the final decision on the partner had been left to their son or daughter. Of those women with children, most (77 (84%)) still had at least one unmarried daughter. Of the 75 women on whom there is information, 29 (39%) wished to choose a future spouse but with their daughter's consent; 25 (33%) were unsure; 18 (24%) said 'whatever is Allah's will'; 2 (3%) said they would leave it to their daughters to choose; and 1 (1%) said they would choose a spouse without their daughter's consent. As an indication of some of the underlying changes in attitudes, of the 66 women providing information, views were divided on whether their daughter should marry in the same way as themselves (27 (41%)) or differently (30 (46%)). Just over one-third of the women (24 (36%)) felt it was reasonable for people to choose their own partners:

"I think that is a good thing. I think if they choose for themselves then they won't break what they have created themselves. It is their life, not ours. If today I choose someone and make her marry that person and tomorrow that breaks up, then her whole life she will blame me. I think it is good if you choose for yourself." (Teraful)

"They can choose for themselves – as long as they make a good choice! But children today don't know the difference between good and bad! As long as they're both happy, that's the main thing." (Fultara)

"In this country that is the way things are happening. This isn't a village where you can force your children to marry someone you choose. You have to give them choice. And they can go out and choose someone for themselves. If that happens what can you do? You are bound to give in to them. You don't have a choice otherwise they will run away." (Nazmin)

A second generation migrant with his elderly uncles in Bangladesh

Some of the women linked changing attitudes with wanting a different future for their daughters:

"I have had such a kick from life, and that has made me wiser. I will get them married when they have finished studying and made something of their lives." (Toslima)

"We would have to ask their consent. They are all studying. They know their own mind. Before parents would get their children married without their consent, and it didn't matter whether they were happy or sad, they had to see it through. Some people are happy in their marriages and others are sad, that's all in Allah's hands. No parent wants to get their child married into a bad home. Every parent wants the best for their child." (Anwara)

"I don't want to get her married young. I will let her study and stand on her own two feet before we get her married." (Shipa)

"I regret getting my eldest daughter married at such a young age. You will still find girls of her age that are unmarried. She has three children now and she is content with what she has, but if she had studied she could have got a good job and maybe her life would have been better. She is happy now, but it could have been different couldn't it?" (Teraful)

However, when asked their opinion of people choosing their own partners, many of the women continued to emphasise the important role played by parents in the decision-making process:

Street posters promoting events for young Bangladeshis

"What can I say about that? It isn't right for our religion or our society because it doesn't allow elders a role. It doesn't give them a voice. It is embarrassing. And for the girl or the boy who gets married in this way, they won't be able to get on in our society either. It takes time for families to heal after situations like that." (Monwara)

"Parents still have an opinion don't they? If they don't have the blessing of their parents would they ever be happy? After Allah it is your parents. They should seek the blessing of their parents. But children today don't understand that." (Neefa)

"It is good in one way and bad in another. If the boy is good and he is from a good family then that is okay. But if she chooses someone who is bad or who is from a bad family, then that is not good. Parents can't be happy with that. But in current times do parents have a choice at all? We are seeing it happen all around us. I hope Allah saves us from such tragedy." (Yasmeen)

"I don't like it. How can they get married without their parents or their in-laws? Anyone who gets married like that will never be welcome at their in-laws house. They will never be happy there. No one will be happy with them, not their parents or their parents-in-law, or the brothers and sisters, or their brother and sisters-in-law." (Beena)

On the other hand, many of the women were keen to stress the benefits of children choosing for themselves:

"I think that is a good thing. It's their life. They are going to have to live it. They are going to have to make their home with that person and share their whole life with them. I think it is good if someone can find a person they can do all that with." (Zaima)

"It is good. If it is a boy or a girl it doesn't matter. If they choose someone and I turn it down and get them married to someone I choose and that marriage doesn't last then where is the good? I think it is better to let them marry someone they choose. If they can make a future together isn't that good?" (Sani)

"If she chose someone we would have to see. Parents only want their children's happiness don't they? If they choose someone and it is someone suitable then of course they can get married. But if they choose a druggie or an alcoholic then no parent would agree, would they? But if it was a good choice then I think that any parent would agree." (Sabera)

"I think it's a good thing. They decide the path of their own lives. When parents choose it's always a gamble. Nobody wants their children to be unhappy, but you can never know. It's not right that parents should arrange a marriage against the wishes of their child, because their child will never be happy. And if their heart isn't in it, then it will be very difficult for them to get along in a new family. It is hard anyway to go to a new family and try and fit in, but if they are unhappy about it, it will be so much harder." (Khayrun)

Some of the women voiced frustrations with their own lives that made them wish for a better future for their daughters:

"It is up to them, to make their own lives. I don't want them to work to give me money. I want them to sort out their own lives. I want them to have a good future. I don't want them to have a life like mine." (Khayrun)

"I always indulge my daughter. I never let her go without because I just want her to be happy. I worry about her having the same fate as me so I don't want to give her any hardship. I always give her what she wants." (Fultara)

This finding is echoed in Kabeer's sample of women in Bangladesh where she reports on a "re-valuing of girl children and the greater willingness on the part of mothers to invest in their education" (2000, p 179). Our evidence suggests that this attitude has almost certainly strengthened in the British context, with women placing considerable emphasis on the need to provide for a better life for their children – daughters as well as sons. The emphasis on education and material fulfilment also needs to be placed within the context of the women's own educational experiences. Twenty-one per cent of those interviewed had received no formal schooling. Of those who had been to school, the mean age of finishing full-time education was 13.5 years. Only 32% of the women could read and write English. Since being in the UK, around one third (37%) had attended courses (English classes in the majority of cases). Many of the women stressed the obstacles to attending these, notwithstanding the advantages:

"I can't really commit to classes because I have to be there for my mother." (Toslima)

"I went to language classes for a while. But not a lot. I couldn't really attend because of the children. I had to drag them along when I went. It was too tiring." (Hajera)

"Yes I would have tried [to go to classes]. I would have gone to school to learn the language. I went once, but then all the time guests would come around. People were always coming by to visit my in-laws. So if someone was coming around, I wouldn't be able to go. I joined the classes, and went as often as I could, but it wasn't that often. I wanted to learn to speak English. But I couldn't learn to do it properly. That's why I say that if parents continue to educate their children, then they will understand that this is really important. If I can speak English then I won't need to take my children or my husband with me, will I [when I go out]? I can do everything myself. It's all for your own good isn't it? If we have this much common sense then why should we object to our children studying and working? And my parents-in-law, they are from a different time, they don't have that sense, they think 'Why should the daughter-in-law go out? What need is there for her to go out? Daughter-in-laws don't go out'." (Saleha)

"I have been thinking a lot recently – I don't know a lot of English. I had one child after another when I came to this country and so I couldn't go to classes. Now there are classes all around me, I could go to these classes and that would improve my life. For example, if someone came to my house to check the electric or the gas, then I couldn't really understand what they were saying. And what if they were lying – and just wanted to come in to steal something. I have to be able to understand what they say. I am happy that I can learn from my own children. The first couple of times I tried they laughed at me because I didn't get the sentence right. But then they realised that I was getting it wrong because I didn't know the right way of saying it and they would help me, and correct it for me. Now they help me all the time when I try to talk to them in English." (Ruji)

"The school was quite far and my mother's health wasn't good and my father was in London so I needed to be at home to help my mother with my young brothers and sisters." (Shebin)

"I have been to English classes. I went for a while, but now I am ill I don't go anymore. I wish I could go, it would keep my mind lighter if I could meet other people. It has been about five or six years since I last went." (Teraful)

Fultara, now separated from her husband, comments:

"My husband wouldn't let me go to classes, he would tell me off and say, 'why do you want to do that? What are you going to do with English?' But what could I do with it now? I couldn't get a job now, could I? Now there are so many young girls looking for jobs. Why would they want to give me a job?"

Younger generation views on marriage

The focus group interviews reinforced the theme of changes in approaches to marriage among the women interviewed in this study. Parveen, a 20-year-

old working for a voluntary organisation, summarises what she sees as the different types of marriage coexisting within the community:

"I see it as three categories. There is the love marriage, the arranged marriage and the Islamic marriage. The love is where you find somebody, do what you please and have a relationship with them before you marry. The arranged marriage is where the girl just turns up on the day, the man just turns up on the day and they're married off. And then there is the Islamic one where ... before the wedding the boy and girl get a chance to talk with the permission of your guardian. And you can talk to him and go out with him with the permission of your guardian. That's the Islamic marriage to me, and that's the one that I go with. Where you have the choice, you get to know them ... your family get to know them. Whereas I think arranged is where you are completely separated from the man, you don't know him, you don't know his family, you don't have a choice."

The group of graduate students felt comfortable with some balance between arranged and an Islamic marriage as interpreted by Parveen. The following exchange illustrates this:

Interviewer:	And what are your views on arranged versus love marriages?
Eva:	Arranged marriages are fine.
Samina:	Yes arranged marriages are fine.
Eva:	I don't see anything wrong with them. If my parents were to introduce me to a whole load of good looking people I'd be happy with that!
Layla:	What can you do? If you haven't found someone let them arrange it.
Seema:	You get some extreme cases, but that's mainly in the Pakistani community.
Eva:	They're really into their back home marriages.
Samina:	They're really into marrying within their rigid structures.
Layla:	My mum had that talk with me, you know, 'If you ever find anyone do come and talk to me about it. Never do anything rash, come and talk to me'.
Eva:	I had the 'Please don't do anything that would embarrass me – your dad would come and kill me!' I was like 'Okay, mum, I'll do my best'.

This same group explained some of the complexities behind discussions with their parents about marriage:

Interviewer: Do they talk to you about marriage?

Layla: Yeah I talk to my mum.

Eva: My mum tells me.... She always tells me about stupid ones they reject, but the more serious ones she tries to keep quiet till they've done their checking out.

Seema: When my older sister got married, I dealt with most of the details. My mum was shy to talk to her and so told me and I told her. But now, because she's so used to talking about marriage with me, she just approaches me directly.

Eva: I think that's good. My sister's got such a big mouth, so when my mum talks about her proposal with me, when I tell her, she just comes in and she's like, 'So where's he from again?' But my mum is used to it now, and so she'll just tell her direct rather than telling her through me.

Seema: I could talk to my mum, but I could never talk to my dad, no way.

Eva and Samina review some of the complexities behind discussions about marriage in the following exchange:

Eva: My dad asked my mum to ask me if I would marry my cousin. So he sat in the next room with the door open while my mum asked me. My mum asked me what I thought of this guy, and I've never met him so I said I didn't care. Then she asked me to marry him. She said 'He's an accountant, he can take care of you. It will solve a lot of problems, because if you marry into the family they will take care of you better'. Then she got frustrated when I said 'No' and she wanted to know my grounds. So I said 'I don't want to have spastic children'. They haven't asked me directly since then, but I've got a feeling they still want me to.

Samina: I can never explain to my parents how genetics work.

Eva: My mother always gives me the examples of 'well these first cousins got married; these first cousins got married'.

Samina: Same with mine. Every time I try to explain to them they say that.

Seema: It's not just that. Nowadays they do see breakdowns in marriages even when they're not related. There are communication problems, where they've married someone from Bangladesh and they've brought them over and it hasn't worked out. So they've seen it. Because my parents have seen it doesn't work they wouldn't really get me married to anyone from back home.

Eva: I think my dad's great idea is 'if she marries him, then they'll look after the land back home, so I won't have to bother so much'. It's in their interest.

Samina: There's a lot of politics.

Eva: There's definitely a lot of politics. I don't understand it.

The focus groups also brought out the view that the extent of 'forced' marriages within the Bangladeshi community had been exaggerated to a significant extent, illustrated by the following exchange:

Sheli: When they use the term 'force', I think it's a way of getting media hype, and making it a big issue.

Jamila: I don't think you can force girls to get married. They can't tie you up and get you married.

Parveen: I don't think girls are forced in that way.... It's just the media. They report one or two cases and make a big deal out of them without really looking into the facts. There are no statistics on forced marriages. It might happen but not as much as the media wants you to believe.

Jamila: A lot of girls are not forced, but its mental pressure: 'We like this boy, because he's from such and such a family, he's got a good job' and so you must like him too. It's not about what's best for you. You don't get the chance to like someone first and then take them to your parents. That's where the difference is. The definition of arranged marriage to me has an element of force in it. But I don't think any parents can physically force their daughter by tying them up or anything.

Parveen: You used to hear about cases where they would take the girl under false pretences to Bangladesh, saying her grandmother was ill. But that doesn't happen anymore.

Jamila: But again, it's never force, because a girl does actually consent in the end. It's force in the sense that the choice wasn't hers, but the act itself wasn't forced.

Sheli: You have to hear it from both sides. There are cases where the marriages have broken down and then they say that they were forced into it. They seem so bitter about it.

Jamila: Before women wouldn't come out of bad marriages. They would think 'If I came out of this marriage what would I do? I would be stuck anyway. So what's the point?' But now because there is help out there that they can access, they are more confident.

Parveen: And before if a woman was divorced it was such a taboo. They were shunned. And now it still exists but nowhere near like it was.

Jamila: And now there are more people who are educated in Islam. And you will get guys who have Islamic knowledge who say 'No, I would like to marry a divorced woman, because of these reasons'. In Islam a divorced woman is not looked down upon. When you marry a divorced woman it's double the reward of marrying a woman who hasn't been divorced before. And so in actual fact that woman is not looked down on at all in Islam.

Parveen: Views are changing now. It's not everywhere but they are changing.

Jamila: It's not everywhere. You still get the odd Bengali family who will say: 'My son's not marrying a divorced girl'. There is still the attitude, but there is the other side that is emerging now.

Sabia and Silma, two of the students from the sixth form college, summarise the changes as follows:

"I think we have more of a say these days. We can meet the guy and decide for ourselves. With our parents they had no choice." (Sabia)

"It's moving away from all of that. Some of my cousins and my sister married out of the Bengali community. And some of them married within the Bengali community but from different areas. Places that my mum would never ever think of getting any of us married. But that is all breaking the mould of 'this family is better than that family' and everyone is mixing." (Silma)

Constraints and losses

The women interviewed had undoubtedly experienced major transformations in their lives; moving continent, raising families, adjusting to the death of children and relatives. Loss was a major theme running through the experiences of what was still a relatively young group of women – 13 had experienced the death of at least one of their children; 17 had lost a husband. As this would suggest, the life course of the respondents had been anything but orderly; rather, there were numerous discontinuities with disruptions caused by famine, illness, political unrest and the sudden death of near kin:

"I can cope with almost everything that happened to me, but not losing my daughter. I just can't forget that. Yesterday I was going to the chemist and I walked past the place she used to play and I could see her running around and playing. Tears just started pouring down my face. And then I saw people looking at me strangely and I just wiped my face and walked on. I thought to myself, I am seeing my daughter here, that's why I am crying. How can any of you know what is going on inside me. When it gets too much for me I just rush to her side in Walthamstow to her graveside." (Toslima)

"I was coming to this country on my own. I came almost straight after the Independence, and at that time Bangladesh didn't have many planes, so the government had to hire one from Pakistan. But the plane crashed near Saudi Arabia somewhere, and nobody would help us because ... the plane was a Pakistani one, and Pakistan said none of their planes had crashed, so the airport official wouldn't believe us, and they hadn't heard of Bangladesh. Then the pilot had to contact Bangladesh, and from there they contacted Pakistan, who told the Arabians what the situation was. We were stuck there for two days. It took me four days to come to this country! I was all on my own, and I had never gone anywhere on my own before! I was a bit scared, but I think that experience made me braver. I have a lot of courage now." (Alima)

"My life has had so many hardships. My husband was a gambler. Even if my sisters are poor, they haven't had to suffer like I have. When I first came here I spent my whole day at the window waiting for him [her husband] to come home, wondering if he would come home. I worried all the way up to his death and I am still worrying. He left me there [in Bangladesh] two months after we got married and I fasted for three months for him. I fasted and prayed to Allah. My future was with my husband and I prayed to Allah to bring him back on the right path. It was only after we had children that he settled down. When he had finally settled down, Allah took him away." (Mariam)

Of the 98 women who responded to an open-ended question on whether they had any worries at the present time, 83 (85%) confirmed that they had, with concerns about children, health and housing being the main themes identified. These worries were expressed in the most poignant way by some of the widows in the study:

"My whole life has gone by worrying about things. I have never known any peace in my heart. I have never had any happiness." (Mariam)

"I am very lonely so you can understand that I feel very bad sometimes. I don't have my husband to share things with. And then I worry about my children too. I worry about their education, their character, their marriages and their future. I just want them to be successful." (Moymun)

"I have so many worries. I worry about the future, how we will get through, how we will eat, what the rest of my life will be like. Where will we get money. I don't have a job, if I tried I couldn't do anything. If I went to English classes I wouldn't be any good. I can't do anything. I have so many worries." (Amina)

The women were asked, in an open-ended question, to say how they would describe their mental state. Many of the women reinforced the impression of an intense preoccupation with worries of different kinds:

"Sometimes I feel that my mind just isn't working. I might go to help my daughter-in-law with the cooking and I will burn the pan and everything without realising it." (Jannat)

"Before I was young I was happy. I didn't even know that sorrow existed. Now I am more unhappy than happy. Now I have found out what stress is and what it can do to you." (Aklima)

"I feel very nervous a lot of the time. It is continuous but I don't know why, and that makes me more nervous! And when you feel that way, you just get more angry. I feel very weak and I get angry at myself for that. I want to be able to do everything for myself but I can't. I find that I am losing patience with everyone much more now. I get annoyed at little things." (Jusna)

Again, some of the comments from the widows were especially bleak and disconcerting:

"It is not good. But what can I do? I am on my own – who will help me? I feel like my heart is shaking. I can't do anything. Who will help me?" (Roshon)

"What can I say? It is as Allah keeps it. I can't find peace of mind." (Rukshana)

"Today I feel as though I am drowning in the middle of the sea. Not one person comes to see me. My mind is very dark, I don't feel like doing anything." (Mariam)

Substantial information on the health status of minority ethnic groups is now available from sources such as the *Health survey for England* (HSE) (Erens et al, 2001). This has confirmed the vulnerability of particular ethnic groups (Pakistanis and Bangladeshis in particular) to long-standing illness and disabilities of various kinds, and the high prevalence of psychiatric illness (reflected in scores on measures such as the General Health Questionnaire). Table 5.1 confirms that on self-assessed health Bangladeshis are much more likely in comparison with other groups

Table 5.1: Self-assessed general health (%)

	Positive			Negative			
	Very good	**Good**	**Total**	**Neither good nor poor**[a]	**Poor**[b]	**Very poor**[c]	**Total**[d]
THS[e]	4	33	**(37)**	11	44	8	**(63)**
HSE[f] (Bangladeshi)	5	37	**(42)**	35	22	1	**(58)**
HSE (Pakistani)	20	30	**(50)**	31	15	4	**(50)**
HSE (Indian)	13	53	**(66)**	25	9	1	**(35)**
HSE (All women)	34	45	**(79)**	15	5	1	**(21)**

[a] 'Neither good nor poor' was the phrasing used in our study as opposed to 'Fair' in the Health Survey for England (HSE).
[b] 'Poor' in our study; 'Bad' in the HSE.
[c] 'Very poor' in our study; 'Very bad' in the HSE.
[d] Percentages may exceed 100 due to rounding up.
[e] Tower Hamlets Survey.
[f] The figures for women from the HSE survey are for those aged 35-54.

to rate their health as poor or very poor. There are differences between the sample in Tower Hamlets and that of the HSE, particularly in relation to the mid-point of the self-assessment. This probably reflects a mixture of the higher level of deprivation in the Tower Hamlets group, and social differences between the Bangladeshi populations sampled (the HSE sample is drawn from the Bangladeshi community across England). Variations in how the question was phrased may also have influenced responses.

The General Health Questionnaire (GHQ12) was also used in the study to test for possible psychiatric illness in the sample of women. The questionnaire is based on 12 questions about general levels of happiness, depression, anxiety and sleep disturbance over the previous four weeks. Following the HSE and other studies, we have taken a score of four or more as an indicator of possible psychiatric disorder. The HSE found a high proportion of Bangladeshis with high GHQ scores. Thirty-two per cent of women aged 35-54 had a score of four or more, compared with 19% among the general population of women in this age group. The score for our respondents was even higher at 39%. Thirty-three per cent of our study scored zero (48% in the HSE for the sample of Bangladeshi women); and 28% scored between one and three (20% in the HSE). Ninety-nine of the women completed the GHQ in our study and answers to individual items are revealing, given some of the previous comments: 42 felt (rather more than usual/much more than usual) under strain; 35 felt unhappy or depressed; 32 felt they were losing confidence in themselves; 22 had

been thinking of themselves as worthless. Some of the pressures are highlighted by the following comments:

"I worry too much. I have so many things to worry about. The house, my husband, the children – how to bring them up as good people. I feel restless all the time." (Sabina)

"I worry ... I just don't know how my headaches are affecting them. They must think 'our mother is a single parent ... she is going through all this'. I don't know how my problems are affecting them. I tell them, you just concentrate on your own work … on your studies. If I am on my own, my mind wanders. I think to myself 'How am I supposed to run such a big family? How will I make all my children into good people? I don't want my children to know how much I worry." (Rupa)

"I worry a lot about my past. I wish I could stop but I can't. If I stop worrying about the past I start worrying about the future. I don't have much confidence in myself anymore. I wish I could move on from all of this but I can't. Sometimes I just don't know what to do." (Fultara)

These findings suggest a vulnerable group of women, having often to cope in isolation, with those separated and widowed facing especially difficult times. The results reinforce Pollen's (2002) observation that even women with extensive local kin may feel isolated, especially when trying to access local health and welfare services. However, a further dimension to the women's lives was the added responsibility of living in a transnational community, which provided supportive ties but at the same time additional responsibilities.

Sustaining transnational relationships

Glick Schiller and her colleagues have defined transnationalism as the process by which:

… immigrants build social fields that link together their country of origin and their country of settlement. Immigrants who build such social fields are designated 'transmigrants'. Transmigrants develop and maintain multiple relations – familial, economic, social, organizational, religious, and political that span borders. Transmigrants take actions, make decisions, and feel concerns, and develop identities within social networks that connect them to two or more societies simultaneously. (1992, p 5)

Paul Thompson and Elaine Bauer, in a study of Jamaican families, emphasise that: "transnationalism is not a figment of the social scientist's imagination, but a reality both in the mind and in practice" (2001, p 14). While Christine Ho (1991), studying Anglo-Trinidadians living in Los Angeles, refers to the "concerted effort to sustain connections across time and geography" among her migrants. Our first generation women maintained a variety of ties with Bangladesh. The majority (79%) had returned on at least one occasion, invariably going with other family members. Visits would often stretch over long periods (49% reported stays lasting between two and four months; 11% had stayed for a period of 10 months or more). The longest visits tended to be around the time when children were of pre-school age. Keeping in touch with relatives, getting children married or seeing a family member who was ill, were identified as the main reasons for returning to Bangladesh. Many of the women mentioned financial or other obstacles preventing them from returning as often as they would like:

"My mother always cries for me to go to Bangladesh all the time. I am the only one of her children in this country. My youngest brother got married a few weeks ago. I couldn't go, how could I go? I can't

afford to take them all and they are all studying." (Neefa)

"I would like to go to Bangladesh again but I don't know if I will. My whole family is there, my parents and brothers and sisters. I am the only one here. But I can't afford to take my children and I can't leave them behind either." (Rong)

"I would like to go back but you need money to go back. Where would I get the money from? I don't even have enough money to pay the bills and eat. How can I go back to Bangladesh?" (Sani)

"I do feel a tug to go back, but how can I go, with so many children? I can't leave them and I can't take them either – where would I get the money from? How much would the fares cost?" (Rupa)

"I have heard that my father is not well in Bangladesh so I have been worrying about him. I feel bad that I don't have the resources to go and see him. He cries on the phone when we speak and I feel as though my heart is breaking." (Halima)

Contacts with mothers were an important part of transnational ties[1]. The majority of the women (71%) still had a mother who was living – in the majority of cases in Bangladesh. Twenty-six of the women reported that their mother's health was 'very good or good', but 31 said it was 'poor or very poor'. A number of the women reported on the tensions created by trying to maintain ties with their mothers:

"After I came here I couldn't keep in touch with her very much. Every four or five months we would write letters. But we never spoke on the phone. I never heard her voice again after leaving Bangladesh [cries]." (Sani)

Interviewer: Where does your mother live?

"America. She lives with my brothers there. She has been there for four years." (Sabera)

Interviewer: Has she come here?

---

[1] For one of the few studies which looks at migration from the perspective of the parents left behind see Miltiades (2002).

"Yes. But she didn't like being in the house all day. In Bangladesh there are more open spaces and it is not like that here. She liked it because we are here, but she didn't like being in the house all day." (Sabera)

"She came and stayed when she was doing her Hajj. But she didn't like it here. It isn't as free as our country is it? You have to rely on other people if you want to go anywhere. So she didn't like staying here." (Asma)

"She lived between this country and Bangladesh. She would go to Bangladesh because she missed my brother's children, but when she was there she would miss us and come back. And when she came back she would start missing them and want to go back again. She didn't have peace in either country. While she was there she missed us, but she couldn't stay a year here before wanting to go back. She died in this country, but we sent her body back to Bangladesh." (Shipa)

There was some evidence from the study of the continuation of remittances from the women to mothers and close family members in Bangladesh. Gardner (1997) suggests that financial flows from London to Sylhet were important in the 1960s and 1970s, when wives and children had yet to migrate. With their arrival, however, remittances gradually dwindled. This research suggested that while generally the case, the pressure to send money home was still an issue for some families. Shuara comments that:

"I occasionally send some money. My heart can't bear it – I always wonder if they are going without: 'are they eating properly? What are they eating?' If I hear they are ill I don't know what to do. I don't have much to give myself. If only I could speak the language I could work. Then I could open the letters from Bangladesh with a light heart, and write back to them and make them happy. Even if I do write to them they are upset – if you don't give them money they don't like you." (Shuara)

Others continued to maintain some support, especially to their mothers:

"If we can we give a bit of money to help with medicines. Sometimes we send money over for her medication or so that they can buy her nice food." (Ruji)

"Sometimes I would send a little money for her." (Yasmeen)

"I send money as often as I can." (Poroush)

Conflict between generations over remittances surfaced in the focus group discussions with younger women. The following extract is from the discussion group with girls at the sixth form college:

London branch of a Bangladeshi bank often used for sending remittances

Interviewer: Do people still send money back to Bangladesh?

Silma: Yes. We've kind of cut it off.

Nusrat: We've cut it off because my brother refused my dad any money to send.

Farhana: That's only because your brother stood up and said no. If it was up to your dad he probably would still be sending money.

Nusrat: He is still sending money. We had a recent drama in our house! My dad is always sending money home to his brother. It's got to the point where it's just ridiculous. Where's the money going? My uncle is supposed to be a successful businessman back home – but where's the money going? My brother really stood up to my dad and said 'I'm not giving you another penny for that man!' My dad got really vexed with my brother and he didn't speak to my brother for two weeks.

Sabia: They just don't realise. You hear about people sending money back to build houses back home, but they don't realise that if our lives are here, and we're trying to build our careers and our lives here, then isn't it better to save the money for yourself?

The following exchange confirms the image of London as a land of wealth and opportunity, reported in the study by Katy Gardner (1997):

Nadia: One of my brothers [from her father's first marriage] is in Bangladesh; he's got a huge business for contracting building work and all of that. And he got two of his daughters married recently and he would write home to my mum and you think 'How stupid is that?' He's writing to this woman who's got kids to look after, who doesn't work, who's living on benefits. He's got businesses and he's got money in Bangladesh so why's he writing to someone here who hasn't got any of that? I could understand a poor person writing and saying 'We haven't got any money and we want to get our daughter married'.

Rahmin: The view that they have in Bangladesh is that London is money. So you can't blame them in that sense because they do honestly believe in their hearts that we are all loaded with money.

Farhana: It's only when they come here that they realise what it's really like.

Nusrat: My mum was talking to someone who just got married and came here and he was saying to my mum 'We never realised it was like this back home. When I was back home we always used to dream of coming here. But having come here now I have just realised how hard it is for you all'. My mum just said he understands and now it's just the matter of explaining it to the rest of the people in Bangladesh.

Silma elaborates on some of the tensions that can develop in families:

"My dad when he was alive. He used to send money home all the time again and again. My mum and dad used to have arguments and arguments. And as children we grew up with hearing that so and so phones and we have to give money. These people don't even know our names and they want us to marry their sons and they want us to send them money. When my dad passed away my mum just said: 'No. I'm not going to give you any more money because believe it or not I need to keep some money for my children. For their sake'. And my mum just cut them off. But for things like Qurbani [second festival in Muslim year] my mum still sends money. She says: 'Whether I live or die we have to send this'. She still gives it. But after my dad died we bought a house here [in Tower Hamlets]. My sister bought it, she said: 'We need to be stable here'. And back home the house that my dad put money into is not ours. My sister said: 'We're strangers back home. Instead of being a stranger in Bangladesh. We should do something here for ourselves'."

The discussion group with women in their twenties also confirmed that money was still being sent back:

Interviewer: Do people still send money back to Bangladesh?

Shipa: Not as much as they used to but sometimes.

Sheli: We have to because we have a home. The way we pay our cousin back is because he is living there, but he is also taking care of everything – land and all that so we don't have to go back all the time when things have to be registered and all that. So we don't always have to keep running back and forth so we maintain their family so that we don't have to worry about things. And when my grandmother isn't well of course we're going to send money back home. Things like that.

Sabina: Occasionally like Eid and somebody's wedding.

Shipa: For zakat you send it for your family to pick out the needy people.

Sheli's family relationship with residual family in Bangladesh describes a common migrant experience, whereby family members in the homeland provide a service managing migrants' assets, which the migrant foresees making use of when they return (Gardner, 2002). On the other hand, this group of young women acknowledged that ties had certainly changed over time:

Interviewer: Can you tell me about how much contact your parents have with Bangladesh?

Parveen: It has certainly decreased. A few years ago it was a constant thing: 'Who's going to Bangladesh, I must give money. And there were calls [from Bangladesh] every other day. But now its decreased. It's odd.

Interviewer: Why do you think that is?

Parveen: I don't know. Maybe because she's busy with other things, she's out there more, she's got her own things to do. Occasionally there's a letter; occasionally there's a call. It's weird. I find it quite strange considering how linked up they were before.

Sheli: For me, it's always been the same. We have a home back in Bangladesh and we've got a cousin who lives there with his family. My grandmother lives there too. And she's my mum's only living parent. So for her the connection is greater. We're always in contact with

what's going on there. She's always going back there. I think it's because of my Nani.

Shipa: Bangladesh has developed also. Okay, its not as far as Britain has, but we got phones. And they can keep in touch on the phone.

Sheli: In the old days they used to write letters and we had to record conversations on tapes so they could hear our voices! They wanted to hear your voice.

Parveen: I think my mum's lost contact because she's confident that they don't need her money, they have their own businesses.

Sabina: My mother is going to Bangladesh more now than when we were young. Before she had to take care of us, but now she's got time to go back. Before it was all around the school holidays. Now she hasn't got that pressure. Most of her family are back there.

The importance, however, of financial ties can be exaggerated. Of greater significance is the nature of transnationalism as a system that binds different cultures. Membership of a transnational community could help individuals retain a sense of belonging and support when relocated to a new country. It could, however, create new difficulties in the form of responsibilities for families divided between the UK and Bangladesh. Some of the younger women interviewed in the study highlighted the tensions this could create for their parents. Sheli, a 26-year-old working in the voluntary sector in Tower Hamlets, comments:

"I don't think our parents feel totally settled if they go back there because they know they've left you behind, so they are still worried about you. I think they're torn between two places all the time."

Parveen, a 20-year-old, also working in the voluntary sector, illustrates the tensions when parents go back to Bangladesh:

"When I was 16, my mum left me and my three sisters and went to Bangladesh and every day she would phone and was crying for us. It was really hard for her. She came back and said she would never do that again until we were all married – there's three more to go and then she can retire to Bangladesh."

The sense of negotiating two societies emerged when mothers talked about the differences between British and Bengali culture. In the following extracts, Khayrun and Nazmin illustrate some of the tensions experienced by the women:

"In our country, young girls didn't go out. There [in Bangladesh] parents wouldn't let them go. Girls don't work in our country. Maybe in the towns they do now, but otherwise they don't. In villages every woman is a 'housewife' even if she isn't married! In this country girls of 17/18 are working outside. And if they are working outside they won't want to come home and work will they? They won't find the time, or they will be too tired. My younger daughters always say, 'When we get older we won't cook all day like you do. You cook every day. When we get older we won't cook rice, we'll get it from a take-away'. It is not better or worse, it is just different. It is different cultures. It is hard for them to try and keep the Bengali culture, because the Bengali culture is to stay at home and cook and look after the family. But in this country you can't just sit at home, can you? They have to go out and work, and then coming home to cook and clean, is just too much isn't it? They can't do everything. It's probably better for them, but it feels strange for people of my age. Everything is too different for us." (Khayrun)

"In this country I can't bring them up exactly the same way as I grew up. There is a different culture here, and they are living in that culture. They need to have both cultures inside them. It is not good for them to become totally English, but then they can't get on in this country if they become totally Bengali. Look at me – what can I do? Nothing, because I don't understand this culture, I can't speak the language. If my daughters were to become like me then they wouldn't be able to do anything with their life. That is why they need both cultures." (Nazmin)

Hajera and Asma emphasise the impact on relationships created by schooling and college education:

"The culture here is different. Here children are all going to school, they are studying. Their minds are different here, it is a different way of thinking. And I have to understand that." (Hajera)

"The most difficult thing is ... in Bangladesh we studied Arabic more, and the Quran. But here with college and the way of life, we can't manage it as well as we did in Bangladesh. In Bangladesh, I was very close with my mother and especially we would pray together at prayer times. That is the most different thing here, we can't all pray together." (Asma)

On the other hand, many of the women in the focus groups confirmed the support received from parents, relating this to the limited opportunities open to first generation migrants, as the following contributions from sixth form students illustrate:

Interviewer:	What are the major differences between your lives and your mothers' lives?
Rhamin:	I think with my mum, she was more restricted than I was. She was married when she was 15 and she came over and had lots of kids. And she couldn't work and she couldn't speak English properly. She did tailoring, she really wanted to broaden her knowledge about England and about the society here. But she couldn't do that because she wasn't able to speak English. And I think she wants that for me – that I should broaden my knowledge and learn whatever I can. So I feel in that sense we are different. She was more restricted than I am.
Silma:	If you look at your mum's life you don't want to live that life because you know you've been given that choice; you can either lead her life or you can lead your own life.
Nadia:	You hear about girls getting married at the age of 16 after doing GCSEs and my mum says to me 'study hard, you don't want to be like that. You don't want to end up at the age of 20 with four children and nothing to do'. And it's encouraging to know that she supports you and she doesn't want you to be like that. I don't think a lot of people see that. My mum has had no purpose to her life – that's how she sees it. I mean

Silma: I think that she's done so much. She's a single mother with four kids. It's just strange that she has so many aspirations for us; it's so nice to know that.

Silma: Our mums don't have qualifications, but we know how strong they are. I look at my mum and I think, she doesn't have to have a degree to be the best mum ever! I know she is. Bringing us up can't have been easy.

Nusrat: My brother had an operation on his stomach a long time ago. My mum was explaining to my sister what it was and she was talking about tissues and things like that and my mum didn't study at all, she only studied till she was 11. How could she know and understand about things like tissues and things in your stomach?

Conclusion: hopes for the future

How did the women we interviewed see their lives unfolding? Now established in Tower Hamlets and with the second half of their lives ahead of them, what hopes did they have for the future? Of the 97 answering this question, 61 (63%) focused on hopes for the future success of their children. For many, the measure of whether migration had been worthwhile rested on the success and accomplishments of their children. The following comments are representative:

"I don't have any hopes for myself. I just want to be able to raise the children well and educate them and make them into decent people." (Shaira)

"That our children don't spend their lives on benefit like us." (Ranu)

"My children's hopes are now my hopes. As long as they are happy, I am happy." (Shipa)

"I measure my life by how my children are doing. Their future is the most important thing for me." (Rohima)

Fourteen women were unable to identify any hope or aspiration for the future; some of these harboured especially negative views about the way ahead:

"What hopes can I have? I have no hopes. I just hope that Allah gives me a quick death." (Shuara, aged 48)

"What hopes can I have – I am going to die soon anyway." (Monwara, aged 39)

"Women's lives are over when they reach 35 or 40. What more of a life do I have?" (Sabina, aged 50)

"My days are going now… they are not coming anymore are they? My days are getting shorter not longer!" (Nazma, aged 41)

"What future? I don't have any future left. Now I am just looking to my children's future." (Zeba, aged 50)

These are striking comments for a group of people that are still comparatively young – at least judged by Western standards. What they reflect, to some degree, is the way their life course had already been marked by changes that for other women (in countries such as Britain) would have spread over a longer period of time. For some of the respondents, marriage, childbirth, migration, divorce, widowhood or chronic ill-health, had been compressed into a short span of time – two decades or less. Change was relentless and holding on to a sense of perspective about the direction in which life was taking them presented major problems for the women.

This last finding points to the relevance of Gardner's comment about the 'emotional' dimension to transnational migration. She found that few of the men and women she interviewed: "… were wholly clear about where they wanted to be, or indeed whether their movement to Britain was a good or bad thing" (2002, p 18). We asked the women in our study to provide a picture of where they saw themselves, looking ahead to five years time. Of the 95 women answering this question, 31 (33%) were unable to give a response and 21 (22%) said there would be no change in their lives. The remainder again focused on aspirations for their children. Makhan, a widow, spoke for many in the sample when she said:

"For us … it's just hopes for the children. The children have grown up here so they have the culture of this country. We as parents have hopes for them. But what they will do and not do in the future … only Allah knows. If Allah allows it … I have many hopes for them."

6

Conclusion and policy recommendations

The final chapter brings together the key policy issues arising from this study of migrant women from Bangladesh. Some of the themes identified in previous chapters have concerned:

- The importance of the transnational context, especially in respect of cultural and social ties.
- The various transitions surrounding migration, for example in relation to marriage and securing a home.
- The establishment of families and households in the context of pressures within the local housing market.
- The important role played by social networks of friends and family.
- Problems associated with poverty and unemployment affecting Bangladeshi households.
- Perceptions of stress and poor health.
- Intergenerational changes and contrasting attitudes among older and younger women.
- The central role of religious beliefs as an anchor in everyday life.
- The high level of aspirations for daughters and sons.

Some of the policy issues arising from these themes can be seen as specific to the Bangladeshi population, reflecting characteristics of their initial migration to the UK. Others, in contrast, are of a more general nature and would be relevant to a range of minority ethnic communities. This chapter begins with the former, examining some the challenges raised by particular features of the Bangladeshi community.

Reconnecting housing and community

The survey data suggests that a number of urgent tasks need to be considered if the lives of Bangladeshi women (and their families) in the UK are to be improved. One important theme from the research (building on studies from Gavron, 1997, and Pollen, 2002, among others), is that the women migrating from Bangladesh in the 1970s and 1980s (and even into the 1990s) never fully recovered from the difficult housing and community environment characteristic of that period. Investment in housing in Tower Hamlets fell by 40% during the 1980s (Hall, 1998), leaving a legacy of acute housing deprivation. At the time this research was starting, some 2,200 households were identified as needing homes with more than four bedrooms. Against this, there were only 1,400 council properties of this size, representing just 5% of the total housing stock. Only a fraction of these larger properties are likely to become available in any one year (London Borough of Tower Hamlets, no date).

The gap that has opened up between housing demand and supply invariably takes its heaviest toll on women in the community, since they shoulder the task of managing households and organising family life. Clearly, this particular issue has been discussed in the public domain for a number of years, in political debates and in reports from independent researchers. The late Peter Shore, former Member of Parliament for Bethnal Green and Stepney, speaking in a parliamentary debate in 1990 on Bangladeshi communities, referred to the 'Dickensian' nature of housing in Tower Hamlets, and the severe overcrowding affecting families[1]. The point was reinforced at the end of the 1990s by Elaine Kempson's (1999) research, which again highlighted the demand for larger properties, but noted as well that these were often located in areas to which people were reluctant to move.

New areas of investment (for example, through the *Estates Renewal Challenge Fund*)[2] are underway which suggest that significant improvements in the housing stock may emerge over the medium and longer term. However, additional approaches will almost certainly be required to meet both immediate needs and to ensure the success of long-term plans. One element here is the case for developing a strategy with a more explicit focus on the needs of large families[3]. At present, most of the policy discussions at a national level emphasise the trend towards a smaller family size, the increase in the proportion of people living alone (at all ages), and the fragmentation of family units with divorce and separation (Allan and Crow, 2001). Bangladeshi families (in Tower Hamlets as elsewhere) cut across these trends and in this way fall into a policy vacuum that reinforces problems arising from the legacy of under-investment in public housing (Rogers and Power, 2000). The first argument, therefore, is for raising the profile of large families as well as acknowledging their role in providing support across different generations. In practical terms, some of the policies that are required would include:

- Targeted funding to support additional financial and social needs among large families.
- The development of specialist support to access the full range of health and welfare provision.
- Positive steps to tackle discrimination and low status.
- Research to identify unmet needs in respect of services and Income Support.

What benefits might accompany an enhanced profile for larger families? In the first place, it might be possible to gain a more accurate measure of their full range of social and housing needs. On the housing front, larger properties may be one solution, but other options may also emerge. Very little is actually known about what women managing large intergenerational households really want in this regard; it is certainly conceivable that they could identify a number of alternatives to meeting their need for good quality housing, of which larger accommodation may be just one of many solutions.

Raising the profile (and status) of large families also has the virtue of opening up a new dimension to the debate on the future of cities, and of the ethnic minority groups within them. Bangladeshis in particular have been described by demographers as an 'encapsulated' community because of their high level of segregation in the urban centres in which they live (Eade et al, 1996). The combination of residential segregation and large family size could be (and often is) viewed in negative terms. However, an opposing view is that 'encapsulation' has a number of virtues when it comes to reconstructing urban environments. Rogers and Power (2000), for example, highlight the problems of inner-city communities faced with declining populations and the flight of the young and ambitious. Tower Hamlets is fortunate in not experiencing either of these problems, in contrast with equivalent communities in the North of England. Young Bangladeshis educated locally – at college or university – are likely to stay and add to the stock of facilities and amenities in the locality. And the population has maintained the expansion that began in the early 1980s, with the concentration of Bangladeshis in inner London increasing rather than decreasing over the 1990s (Scott et al, 2001).

The key issue arising from this is how to link the advantages of encapsulation, notably with its creation of what Putnam (2000) refers to as 'bonding social

---

[1] House of Commons Debate, *Hansard*, cols 1358-1364, 20 July 1990.

[2] DTLR, News Release, 24 March 2000. See also THNDC (2000). Ambrose and MacDonald (2001), however, argue from their research on the Ocean and Limehouse estates, that urban regeneration in areas such as inner London can lead to rent increases and a rise in levels of debt. This is likely to cause particular problems for Bangladeshi families, given high unemployment and large family size.

[3] This may of course be time-limited, given the decline in fertility among second and later generation Bangladeshis (Berthoud, 2000).

capital'[4], with the demand for large-scale urban renewal. Put differently, it might be argued that urban renewal is unlikely to happen if we fail to recognise the positive aspects of 'segregated' neighbourhoods. For example, they may offer the best prospect in the short term for realising the model of 'sustainable communities' as advocated by Richard Rogers (1997) in his book *Cities for a small planet*. Here, he puts forward the case for redeveloping derelict and brownfield sites (which cover 5% of inner London) with dense, mixed developments combining shops, workplaces and schools. Many of these are in fact beginning to take place within the Bangladeshi community, but their potential for revitalising derelict areas is insufficiently recognised or supported. Yet, as Putnam points out in his definition of bonding social capital: "Dense networks in ethnic enclaves ... provide crucial social and psychological support for less fortunate members of the community, while furnishing start-up financing, markets, and reliable labour for entrepreneurs" (2000, p 22). The advantages of these elements clearly need to be built on, while at the same time developing so-called 'bridging' forms of social capital that can provide improved linkages between groups within the community and resources beyond it. This may be especially important for those such as first generation migrant women, who although often members of strong social networks may be relatively isolated in accessing help and support at times of crisis.

Achieving urban regeneration in the broadest sense is also important in respect of women's physical safety in moving around the inner city. As noted in Chapter 4, worries about being mugged or robbed surfaced in many of the interviews, and most of the women confirmed that they would feel unsafe going out after dark[5]. Such fears undoubtedly contributed to another finding from the research, namely, the way in which respondents contrasted the physical restrictions of urban living with the 'openness' of

village life in Bangladesh (see also, Gardner, 2002). Yet much of this may be attributed to the way in which public space on many of the estates and on the streets was dominated by youths, gangs and associated male subcultures. Campbell (1993, p 320) sees this as part of the "erosion of *co-operative* use of public space", with groups such as women and older people subject to a range of restrictions. In policy terms, this suggests the need for a coalition, based around different age and ethnic groups, to challenge the way that urban space is partitioned and controlled by sectional (often male) interests. Progress in this area may have a positive effect in improving the quality of life of groups such as women, children and older people.

Promoting various forms of community development is therefore one important dimension to the concerns of Bangladeshi families. A more immediate issue, however, concerns practical interventions to improve the quality of the housing environment – an issue of major concern, given a typical household size of six or more people. Our respondents highlighted worries about the problem of damp affecting flats and houses (with potential health consequences for children), difficulties in getting repairs carried out, and lack of access to secure outside space. Not all of these problems have immediate solutions, but some, such as improving the response time to requests for repairs, are achievable in the short term. Other issues, such as tackling overcrowding, will require a more strategic response, especially in terms of more effective management of the existing housing stock. Some of the key areas identified in the study by Kempson (1999) include:

- freeing up under-occupied properties for use by larger households;
- more sensitive allocation of housing;
- adapting some of the existing housing stock to create larger houses.

Language skills

During the period of this research, there was much public debate about the failure of migrants settling in the UK to acquire skills in spoken and written

---

[4] Putnam views bonding social capital as a form of "sociological superglue ... creating strong in-group loyalty" (2000, p 22). Bridging networks, in contrast, are better for "linkage to external assets and for information diffusion".

[5] This confirms the findings of research among older people in Bethnal Green (Phillipson et al, 2001) and in Newham (Scharf et al, 2002).

English[6]. Our research appears to provide some confirmation of this point: only one third of the women interviewed said they could read and write English, and even this group reported these skills to be limited in scope. However, our research also found many of the women expressing frustration at their inability to communicate in English. Many reported problems in attending classes in the context of raising a large family or having other caring responsibilities, or being given hostility within their own family (sometimes from their spouse). Many of the women, having now completed their families, expressed enthusiasm both to learn English and to tackle other subjects. We regard this as an important finding, one that goes some way to clarifying current debates about the role of language in respect of minority ethnic groups. In policy terms, it underlines the valuable role within the local area of organisations such as Toynbee Hall and the Tower Hamlets Parents Centre, in their provision of language classes and related services for groups inside the Bangladeshi community[7]. Our research strongly underlines the value (and local demand) for this kind of provision and the need for core funding to support such services.

The obstacles to the take up of literacy schemes should not, however, be underestimated. A high proportion of women reported that they lacked confidence when approaching educational providers – hardly surprising given that for some women their last experience of a classroom may have been in a village school some 30 years previously. Plus the sheer pressure of day-to-day tasks within the home tends to make educational development a secondary issue. Such factors reinforce the need for highly skilled and well-trained educational workers to engage with the community, and to tackle the obstacles that the women in this study identified. Blaming the migrant should be replaced by tackling

---

[6] The various strands to this discussion are summarised by Paul Kelso, *The Guardian*, 27 October 2001.

[7] Toynbee Hall organises a Home Literacy Project targeted at young Bangladeshi women. The Tower Hamlets Parents Centre has among its objectives that of providing "... advice, education and training for parents to empower them to discharge their duties as parents, and to encourage active parental participation in their children's education" (Tower Hamlets Parents Centre, Annual Report, 1998/99).

the reasons why people find it difficult to access educational provision in the first place.

Migration and social policy

Another issue arising from the research concerns the absence of a social policy to support migrants fresh to the UK. The research demonstrates the way that women – often with no direct experience of the complexities of an urban environment – were often left to struggle to adapt as best they could. Many were part of social networks that could provide support and advice, but not everyone was so fortunate and for those without, major problems could be experienced. This might have been less serious if it was just women and their partners alone. In most cases, however, it involved children (and occasionally older relatives) and hence the need to access a wide range of health, social and educational organisations.

This experience undoubtedly places a premium on specialist services such as those offering welfare rights advice and support. Our interviews confirm that migrants are likely to draw heavily on help of this kind. In some respects, this should be seen as a 'preventive/proactive' service with a particular focus on the needs of new migrants. Interviews with the respondents suggest there is much to be gained from guiding people into the network of available services at the first opportunity. Most of the women, at the time of the interview, were carrying heavy responsibilities in respect of care work across different generations. Orchestrating (and accessing) the range of potential services able to offer support would test those with extensive knowledge of the welfare system. For our respondents, the danger of missing out on basic income or welfare supports was additionally high (Widows Benefit was one example from this research).

This last observation suggests the need both to extend existing services in areas such as welfare rights advice, but also to consider innovative forms of assistance that can join different parts of the social security, education and employment systems. The development of specialist posts within local authorities such as Tower Hamlets, charged with utilising a broad swathe of current statutory and voluntary provision, might be one approach to consider. Such posts, if sufficiently grounded within the community, could develop new approaches to building on the strengths of existing social networks, as well as developing new forms of service provision. Supporting voluntary organisations campaigning for the rights of women will also be important, as these may offer the most direct route to responding to needs and issues as they arise.

There is also an intergenerational dimension to the issue of assisting the adjustment of first generation migrants. This research has demonstrated that much is being achieved in cooperative ties between first and later generations. First generation migrants may take initial, hesitant steps in English through help from sons and daughters; they may also gain new contacts (from outside the Bangladeshi community) from the friends of their children; and their own attitudes will be changed and challenged by children born and educated in the UK. Doubtless they will also take note of the way in which their own children wrestle with complex issues relating to social identity. The 100 women in the study viewed themselves as Muslims and Bengalis; the younger women in the focus groups were more likely to see themselves in terms of a variation on an Asian/Muslim/British theme. The older women retained close emotional ties with Bangladesh (unsurprising given that most had mothers living in that country); the younger women had more distant attitudes (as reflected in their views on remittances). These generational connections are, however, being debated and changed in numerous ways (most notably in the area of marriage) and require more understanding and acknowledgement than is presently the case.

Migration and the new citizenship

A final set of issues concern the relationship between the Bangladeshi women interviewed in this study, and wider debates on the theme of citizenship and social justice (Soysal, 1994; Castles and Davidson, 2000; Turner, 2001). The changing nature of citizenship goes some way in explaining many of the difficulties that seemed to affect the lives of our respondents. As observed in Chapter 5, this was a group with considerable anxieties and worries about various aspects of their lives: their relatives in another continent; the future of their children; attitudes encountered on the street; their own mental and

physical health. These worries were very real for a group with the everyday pressures of managing a home on a limited financial budget, but they also reflected insecurities about place and identity in a globalised world. Ulrich Beck argues that: "People are expected to live their lives with the most diverse and contradictory transnational and personal identities and risks" (2000, p 169). While Martin Albrow makes the point that: "Under globalised conditions it becomes less easy for individuals to affirm their identity within the strict confines of nation, gender, age or any other categorical distinctions" (1996, p 151).

Our respondents were coping both with the dislocation and the new opportunities created by crossing continents. Levitt, in her study of Dominican migrants to the USA, refers to the way in which the lives of her respondents were no longer bound by national borders. Developing this argument, she goes on to make the following point:

> They do not shift their loyalties and participatory energies from one country to another. Instead, they are integrated, to varying degrees, into the countries that receive them, at the same time that they remain connected to the countries that they leave behind. Citizenship is only one of several bases upon which individuals form their identities or exercise their rights. (Levitt, 2001, p 5)

In the British context, one implication of our research is that social policy, as a set of arrangements framed within the nation state, should have a more explicit 'transnational' dimension than is presently the case. First and later generation migrants will almost certainly continue to be active in their countries of origin (remittances being only one aspect of a broad field of social, cultural and economic exchange). Cross-cultural social networks will continue to thrive, sustained through the expanded possibilities introduced by new technology (Vertovec, 2001). The key issue, however, is the extent to which these additional elements of citizenship are given due acknowledgement in the countries to which people migrate. The argument here is that without such recognition, new forms of social exclusion may appear and full participation in society compromised. In this context, our respondents challenge the relevance of traditional approaches to citizenship. Delanty (2000, p 126), in his review of perspectives arising from the work of T.H. Marshall, suggests that the classic model of national citizenship brought together four main components: rights, responsibilities, participation and identity. In a globalised world, however, these elements undergo a significant degree of fragmentation. In relation to political identity, Delanty concludes:

> [The] ... challenge ... [is] to respond to the internal fragmentation of citizenship and the emergence of a multi-levelled polity in which democracy operates at different levels and according to different models. Rather than locating democratic citizenship at one level, it must be seen as operating on the subnational, national and transnational levels. (2000, p 136)

Failure to respond to the changing basis of citizenship invariably affects some groups more than others. Castles and Davidson (2000) clarify this point in their distinction between *access to citizenship* and *substantial citizenship*. The former is symbolised by the granting of a passport in the country of residence; the latter by equal chances of participation in various areas of society such as politics, work, welfare systems and cultural relations. The women in our study have managed the former, but were some way from achieving the latter. To some degree this reflected problems with social policy in its traditional guise, for example difficulties in accessing benefits, the impact of urban deprivation and poor quality housing. However, it also reflected societal ambivalence concerning membership of a transnational community in which relationships and personal identities are more fluid and mobile in their construction.

One response to these issues might be to move towards what Delanty (2000) refers to as 'cosmopolitan citizenship'. Cosmopolitanism is an important philosophical idea to consider in as much as it offers the basis for combining concerns about social exclusion with ideas about new forms of participation. Andrew Linklater (1998) cites Beitz's view that the essence of cosmopolitanism arises from the belief that all human beings possess equal moral standing. Linklater argues that cosmopolitanism suggests that political communities should widen their ethical horizons until the point is reached where no individual or group interest is systematically excluded from moral consideration. He goes on to suggest that:

> ... cosmopolitan citizenship enlarges the social realm in which the achievements of national citizenship influence human conduct. The duties of national citizens require collective action to improve the life-chances of the unjustly excluded and to increase their level of autonomy within the nation-state. Cosmopolitan citizenship requires joint action to ameliorate the condition of the most vulnerable groups in world society and to ensure that they can defend their legitimate interests. (Linklater, 1998, pp 206-7)

This form of citizenship could have at least two beneficial consequences within the context of the findings of our research. First, the limitations of national citizenship in countering inequalities within the Bangladeshi population could be challenged by the moral vision implicit in the cosmopolitan view. In this sense, the failure to remedy material deprivation is not solely redistributive but is also about local and community-wide perceptions (and stereotypes) about the nature of (in this instance) Muslim/Islamic groups. A cosmopolitan view, however, underlines the responsibilities of different communities in responding to the needs of vulnerable groups. In the present climate, however, this will require more effective forms of communication if needs are to be fully articulated and recognised. Second, there is much to be gained (as identified in the previous quotation) from widening the 'social realm' around which citizenship is constructed. Promoting effective social inclusion for the Bangladeshi community must, as already argued, include a clearer sense of the 'transnational' dimension to their lives. The danger at present is that this is viewed as marginal rather than representing a core element in the construction of identity. In this way the key elements of what Castles and Davidson (2000) refer to as 'substantial citizenship' will continue to be neglected, thus contributing to the maintenance of inequality between Bangladeshis and other ethnic minority groups. The danger and dilemma for the women in this study is that their lives are divided across different cultural settings. As Gardner states: "For many women transnational migration means that they are continually split between their need to be with people in different places" (2002, p 128). Our findings suggest that this can create a chronic sense of insecurity for women, an experience that must be addressed through the redefinition of citizenship to suit the realities of a more mobile world.

Conclusion

This research has attempted to shed light on an important but neglected group within the ethnic minority community in the UK. The claim made for this study is relatively modest: Bangladeshis are a small group within the total ethnic minority population in the UK; Bangladeshis in Tower Hamlets are themselves distinctive in many respects; and our concern has been solely with the women in this group in their prime years of raising and caring for their families. And, of course, life is changing inside the community: fertility rates are declining; children (daughters especially) are increasingly successful in further and higher education; and many are moving into professional jobs vastly different to the first generation's experiences of long hours in the restaurant trade and heavy industry. However, many issues and concerns still exist, and the problems facing the women interviewed for this study must come high on any list of priorities.

The depth of social exclusion illustrated by inadequate housing, poor health and low incomes, underlines the case for an urgent, targeted response within social policy. Plus a more effective set of supports needs to be considered for migrants who, despite the existence of well-developed social networks, may be alienated by the pace of change of an urban culture. Bangladeshis may, of course, be exceptional in many respects. However, it seems inconceivable that by, say, the middle of the 21st century, the East End will not still be doing what it has done for hundreds of years: namely providing a new home for groups in search of refuge or improving their lives. Our research, if it is at all generalisable, suggests that help for such people remains inadequate. The task, then, is to make migration a less distressing and disruptive experience than is presently the case. The argument of this study is that this should be viewed as an important goal for social and economic policy in a globalised world.

References

Ackroyd, P. (2000) *London: The biography*, London: Chatto and Windus.

Ackroyd, P. (2001) 'The city', in *The Observer Supplement*, 28 January.

Adams, C. (1987) *Across seven seas and thirteen rivers*, London: THAP Books.

Ahmed, N., Phillipson, C. and Latimer, J. (2001) *Transformations of womanhood through migration*, Centre for Social Gerontology, Working Paper No 8, Keele: Keele University.

Albrow, M. (1996) *The global age*, Cambridge: Polity Press.

Allan, G. and Crow, G. (2001) *Families, households and society*, London: Palgrave.

Ambrose, P. and MacDonald, D. (2001) *For richer, for poorer?*, Brighton: The Health and Social Policy Research Centre, University of Brighton.

Ballard, R. (ed) (1994a) *Desh Pardesh: The South Asian presence in Britain*, London: Hurst and Company.

Ballard, R. (1994b) 'Introduction: The emergence of Desh Pardesh', in R. Ballard (ed) *Desh Pardesh: The South Asian presence in Britain*, London: Hurst and Company, pp 1-34.

Ballard, R. (2001) *The impact of kinship on the economic dynamics of transnational networks: Reflections on some South Asian developments*, Center for Migration and Development Working Paper Series, Princeton, NJ: Princeton University Press.

Barot, R., Bradley, H. and Fenton, S. (1999) 'Rethinking ethnicity and gender', in R. Barot, H. Bradley and S. Fenton (eds) *Ethnicity, gender and social change*, London: Macmillan, pp 1-25.

Basch, L., Schiller, N. and Blanc-Szanton, C. (1994) *Nations unbound: Transnational projects, post-colonial predicaments and de-territorialised nation-states*, Langhorne, PA: Gordon and Breach.

Beck, U. (2000) 'Living your own life in a runaway world: individualisation, globalisation and politics', in W. Hutton and A. Giddens (eds) *On the edge*, London: Jonathan Cape, pp 164-75.

Becker, G. (1997) *Disrupted lives: How people create meaning in a chaotic world*, Berkeley, CA: University of California Press.

Berthoud, R. (2000) *Family formation in multi-cultural Britain: three patterns of diversity*, Institute for Social and Economic Research, Working Paper 2000-34, Essex: University of Essex.

Brah, A. (1996) *Cartographics of Diaspora: Contrasting identities*, London: Routledge.

Burholt, V., Wenger, C., Scott, A., Yalta, B. and Roy, S. (2000) 'Bangladeshi immigration to the UK: older people's support networks in the sending and receiving countries', *Quality in Ageing*, vol 1, no 2, pp 18-30.

Campbell, B. (1993) *Goliath: Britain's dangerous estates*, London: Methuen.

Carter, C. and McGoldrick, M. (1998) *The expanded family life cycle*, New York, NY: Allyn and Bacon.

Castles, S. and Davidson, A. (2000) *Citizenship and migration*, London: Macmillan.

Castle, S., Korac, M. and Vasta, E. (2001) *Integration: Mapping the field*, Synopsis of a report by the Centre for Migration and Policy Research and Refugee Studies Centre, University of Oxford, London: Institute of Public Policy Research Seminar Series on the Future of Migration.

Choudhury, Y. (1993) *Roots and tales of the Bangladeshi settlers*, Birmingham: Sylhet Social History Group.

Cornwell, J. (1984) *Hard earned lives*, London: Tavistock.

Corrigan, P. (1979) *Schooling the smash street kids*, London: Macmillan.

Crow, G., Allan, G. and Summers, M. (2001) 'Changing perspectives on the insider/outsider distinction in community sociology', *Community, Work and Family*, vol 4, no 1, pp 29-48.

Dale, A., Shaeen, N., Kalra, V. and Fieldhouse, E. (2001a) *Routes into education and employment for young Pakistani and Bangladeshi women in the UK*, Working Paper No 10, ESRC Future of Work Programme, CCSR, Manchester: University of Manchester.

Dale, A., Shaeen, N., Kalra, V. and Fieldhouse, E. (2001b) *The Labour market prospects for Pakistani and Bangladeshi women*, Working Paper no. 11, ESRC Future of Work Programme, CCSR, Manchester: University of Manchester.

Delanty, G. (2000) *Citizenship in a global age*, Buckingham: Open Press University.

DeLaet, D. (1999) 'Introduction: the invisibility of women in scholarship on international migration', in G. Kelson and D. DeLaet (eds) *Gender and immigration*, London: Macmillan, pp 1-24.

Desai, P. (2000) 'Spaces of identity, cultures of conflict: the development of new British Asian masculinities', Unpublished PhD thesis, University of London.

Dutt, G.C. (1995) *Health care for Bangladeshis abroad*, London: Ruposhi Bangla.

Eade, J. (1997a) 'Keeping the options open: Bangladeshis in a global city', in A. Kershen (ed) *London: the promised land? The migrant experience in a global city*, Aldershot: Avebury, pp 91-109.

Eade, J. (1997b) 'Identity, nation and religion: educated young Bangladeshis in London's East End', in J. Eade (ed) *Living the global city*, London: Routledge, pp 127-45.

Eade, J. (1999) 'Roots and routes: British Bengalis and questions of Homeland', in S. Weil (ed) *Routes and routes: Ethnicity and migration in global perspective*, Jerusalem: The NCJW Research Institute for Innovation in Education.

Eade, J., Vamplew, T. and Peach, C. (1996) 'The Bangladeshis: the encapsulated community', in C. Peach (ed) *Ethnicity in the 1991 Census, vol 2, The Ethnic Minority Populations of Britain*, London: Office for National Statistics, pp 150-60.

Erens, B., Primatesta, P. and Prior, G. (eds) (2001) *Health survey for England: The health of minority ethnic groups '99* (2 volumes), London: Office for National Statistics.

Evandrou, M. (2000) 'Ethnic inequalities in health in later life', *Health Statistics Quarterly*, Winter, pp 20-8.

Faist, T. (2000) *The volume and dynamics of international migration and transnational social spaces*, Oxford: Clarendon Press.

Gardner, K. (1995) *Global migrants, local lives*, Oxford: Clarendon Press.

Gardner, K. (1997) 'Identity, age and masculinity amongst Bengali elders in East London', in A. Kershen (ed) *A question of identity*, Aldershot: Avebury, pp 160-78.

Gardner, K. (1998) 'Death, burial and bereavement amongst Bengali Muslims in Tower Hamlets, East London', *Journal of Ethnic and Migration Studies*, vol 24, no 3, pp 507-21.

Gardner, K. (2002) *Age, narrative and migration*, Oxford: Berg.

Gardner, K. and Shukur, A. (1994) 'I'm Bengali: I'm Asian, and I'm living here: the changing identity of British identities', in R. Ballard (ed) *Desh Pardesh: The South Asian presence in Britain*, London: Hurst and Company, pp 142-64.

Gavron, K. (1997) 'Migrants to citizens, changing orientations among Bangladeshis of Tower Hamlets', London: Unpublished PhD thesis, University of London.

Ginn, J. and Arber, S. (2001) 'Pension prospects of minority ethnic groups: inequalities by age and gender', *Sociology*, vol 52, no 3, pp 519-39.

Glick Schiller, N., Basch, L. and Blanc-Szantoni, C. (eds) (1992) *Towards a transnational perspective on migration*, New York, NY: New Academy of Sciences.

Gulati, L. (1994) *In the absence of their men*, New Delhi: Sage Publications.

Hall, P. (1998) *Cities in civilisation*, London: Weidenfeld and Nicolson.

Hartmann, B. and Boyce, J. (1979) *Needless hunger: Voices from a Bangladeshi village*, San Francisco, CA: Institute for Food and Development Policy.

HEA (Health Education Authority) (2000) *Black and minority ethnic groups in England: The second health and lifestyles survey*, London: HEA.

Ho, C. (1991) *Salt-water trinnies: Afro-Trinidadian immigrant networks and non-assimiliation in Los Angeles*, New York, NY: AMS Press.

Hochschild, A. (2000) 'Global care chains and emotional surplus value', in W. Hutton and A. Giddens (eds) *On the edge: Living with global capitalism*, London: Jonathan Cape, pp 130-46.

Hoerder, D. (2001) 'Reconstructing life courses: a historical perspective on migrant experiences', in V. Marshall, W. Heinz, H. Kruger and A. Verma (eds) *Restructuring work and the life course*, Toronto: University of Toronto Press.

Kabeer, N. (2000) *The power to choose: Bangladeshi women and labour market decisions in London and Dhaka*, London: Verso.

Kalb, D., van der Land, M., Staring, R., van Steenbergen, B. and Wilterdink, N. (eds) (2000) *The ends of globalisation: Bringing society back in*, Oxford: Rowman and Littlefield.

Kempson, E. (1999) *Overcrowding in Bangladeshi housing*, London: Policy Studies Institute.

Kershen, A. (2000) 'Mother tongue as a bridge to assimilation? Yiddish and Sylheti in East London', in A. Kershen (ed) *Language, labour and migration*, Aldershot: Ashgate, pp 11-38.

Khanum, S.M. (1994) 'We just buy illness in exchange for hunger: experiences of health care, health and illness among Bangladeshi women in Britain', Unpublished PhD thesis, Keele: Keele University.

Khanum, S.M. (2001) 'The household patterns of a "Bangladeshi village", in England', *Journal of Ethnic and Migration Studies*, vol 27, no 3, pp 489-504.

Kolenda, P. (1968) 'Region, caste and family structure: a comparative study of the Indian "joint" family', in M. Singer and C. Bernard (eds), *Structure and change in Indian society*, Chicago, IL: Aldine.

Land, H. (1969) *Large families in London*, Occasional Papers in Social Administration No 32, London: Bell.

LBTH (London Borough of Tower Hamlets) (no date) *People and profile*, London: LBTH.

Levitt, P. (2001) *The transnational villagers*, Berkeley, CA: University of California Press.

Linklater, A. (1998) *The transformation of political community*, Cambridge: Polity Press.

Miltiades, H. (2002) 'The social and psychological effect of an adult child's emigration on non-immigrant Asian Indian parents', *Journal of Cross-Cultural Gerontology*, vol 17, pp 33-55.

Modood, T., Berthoud, R., Lakey, J., Nazroo, J., Smith, P., Virdee, S. and Beishon, S. (1997) *Ethnic minorities in Britain: Diversity and disadvantage*, London: Policy Studies Institute.

Nazroo, J. (1997) *The health of Britain's ethnic minorities*, London: Policy Studies Institute.

Papastergiadis, N. (2000) *The turbulence of migration*, Cambridge: Polity Press.

Phillipson, C., Al-Haq, E., Ullah, S. and Ogg, J. (2000) 'Bangladeshi families in Bethnal Green: older people, ethnicity and social exclusion', in T. Warnes, L. Warren and M. Nolan (ed) *Care services for later life*, London: Jessica Kingsley, pp 273-90.

Phillipson, C., Bernard, M., Phillips, J. and Ogg, J. (2001) *The family and community life of older people: Social networks and social support in three urban areas*, London: Routledge.

Phizacklea, A. (1999) 'Gender and transnational migration', in R. Barot, H. Bradley and S. Fenton (eds) *Ethnicity, gender and social change*, London: Macmillan, pp 29-45.

PIU (Performance and Innovation Unit) (2001) *Ethnic minorities and the labour market: Interim analytical report*, London: Cabinet Office.

Pollen, R. (2002) 'Bangladeshi family life in Bethnal Green', Unpublished PhD thesis, University of London.

Porter, R. (1994) *London: A social history*, London: Hamish Hamilton.

Portes, A. (2000) 'Globalisation from below: the rise of transnational communities', in D. Kalb, M. van der Land, R. Staring, B. van Steenbergen and N. Wilterdink (eds) *The ends of globalisation: Bringing society back in*, Oxford: Rowman and Littlefield, pp 253-70.

Portes, A. and Bach, R. (1985) *Latin journey: Cuban and Mexican immigrants in the United States*, Berkeley, CA: University of California Press.

Putnam, R. (2000) *Bowling alone: The collapse and revival of American Community*, New York, NY: Simon and Schuster.

Qureshi, T. (1998) *Living in Britain: Growing old in Britain*, London: Centre for Policy on Ageing.

Rogers, R. (1997) *Cities for a small planet*, London: Faber Books.

Rogers, R. and Power, A. (2000) *Cities for a small country*, London: Faber Books.

Ross, E. (1983) 'Survival networks: women's neighbourhood sharing in London before World War One', *History Workshop Journal*, Spring, pp 4-27.

Scott, A., Pearce, D. and Goldblatt, P. (2001) 'The sizes and characteristics of the minority ethnic populations of Great Britain – latest estimates', *Population Trends*, no 105, Autumn, pp 6-15.

Scharf, T., Phillipson, C., Smith, A.E. and Kingston, P. (2002) *Growing older in socially deprived areas*, London: Help the Aged.

Silveira, E.R.T. and Ebrahim, S. (1998) 'A comparison of mental health among minority ethnic elders and whites in East and North London', *Age and Ageing*, vol 27, no 3, pp 375-83.

Soysal, Y. (1994) *Limits of citizenship: Migrants and postnational membership in Europe*, Chicago, IL: University of Chicago Press.

Taylor, W. (2001) *This bright field*, London: Methuen.

THNDC (Tower Hamlets New Deal for Communities) (2000) *The Ocean Estate delivery plan, 2000-2010*, London: THNDC.

Thompson, P. and Bauer, E. (2000) 'Jamaican transnational families: points of pain and sources of resilience', *Wadabagei: A Journal of the Caribbean and its Diaspora*, vol 3, pp 1-37.

Tower Hamlets Parent's Centre *Annual Report 1998/ 99*, London: THPC

Turner, B. (2001) 'The erosion of citizenship', *British Journal of Sociology*, vol 52, no 2, pp 189-209.

Vertovec, S. (1999) 'Conceiving and researching transnationalism', *Ethnic and Racial Studies*, vol 22, no 2, pp 447-62.

Vertovec, S. (2000) 'Religion and Diaspora', Paper presented at the conference on New Landscapes on Religion in the West, Oxford University.

Vertovec, S. (2001) *Transnational social formations: Towards conceptual cross-fertilization*, Center for Migration and Development Working Paper Series, Princeton, NJ: Princeton University Press.

Werbner, P. (1990) *The migration process: Capital, gifts and offerings among British Pakistanis*, Oxford: Berg.

Werbner, P. (2002) *Imagined diasporas among Manchester muslims*, Oxford: James Currey.

Westwood, S. and Phizacklea, A. (2000) *Transnationalism and the politics of belonging*, London: Routledge.

Widgery, D. (1991) *Some lives! A GP's East End*, London: Sinclair-Stevenson.

Young, M. and Willmott, P. (1957) *Family and kinship in East London*, London: Pelican Books.

Zorlu, A. (2001) *Ethnic minorities in the UK: Burden or benefit*, Working Paper 2001-14, Colchester: Institute for Social and Economic Research, University of Essex.

Appendix A: Study leaflet

NUFFIELD FOUNDATION RESEARCH PROJECT

KEELE UNIVERSITY

BANGLADESHI WOMEN: MIGRATION AND IDENTITY

Despite extensive research about the Bangladeshi community, there is still limited knowledge about the lives of Bangladeshi women, especially those in the 35-55 age group.

These women have an important position in the household, with multiple responsibilities as mother, carer and housekeeper. However, the majority are likely to have limited contact with service providers and the full extent of their various responsibilities remain unclear.

The research project aims to study the experiences of this group of women, and to provide an insight into:

* **Their roles within the home and community.**
* **Their relationships within the family, in particular with their daughters.**
* **Their experiences in relation to care provision, support networks and mental health.**

Information will be collected from a sample of Bangladeshi women living in Tower Hamlets, utilising in-depth interviews and focus groups. The interviews will explore women's lives before and after migration, their present situation in the community, and their hopes and aspirations for the future for themselves and their families.

A younger group of women aged 16-25 will also be interviewed to allow for comparisons across generations. The nature of the mother-daughter tie will be a specific feature of these interviews. The interview will also explore their experience of life in Tower Hamlets and their own aspirations for the future.

For more information on this project please contact:

Nilufar Ahmed on 020 7882 3629 or email n.ahmed@appsoc.keele.ac.uk

Production and design: NANUAG Tel: 020 8475 0422 www.nanua.co.uk

---

বাংলাদেশী মহিলা: অভিবাসন ও পরিচয়

আপনি কি ৩৫-৫৫ বছর বয়সী বাংলাদেশী মহিলা?

নিলুফার আহমেদ, ফোন: 020 7882 3629

Production and design: NANUAG Tel: 020 8475 0422 www.nanua.co.uk

Appendix B:
Questionnaire form

Outcome

Interview completed	8
Wrong age	9
Refused	A
No contact	B
Other (write in and code)	D

Contact details

Name _____   District _____

Address _____

_____

_____

Comments

Name of interviewer: _____

Start time: _____

Finish time: _____

Bangladeshi women: Migration and identity

Contents

Nuffield Foundation Research Project
Keele University, School of Social Relations in collaboration with Cardiff University

Time interview started:

Section A: Experience of migration

A1a   Could you tell me the year in which you came to live in the UK?
      (Probe: May be different to when respondent first visited)

      Enter year
      (Give estimate if necessary)

A1b   Could I just check how old you were when you finally left Bangladesh?
      Enter age in years

A1c   And could I just check, how old are you now?
      Enter age in years

A2   What do you remember of your feelings about leaving Bangladesh?

A3   Which part of Bangladesh did you come from?
      (Probe: Is this the city/town/village in which you were born?)

A4   Would you describe ... [name of area] as rural or urban?

A5   Who brought you to the UK?

Spouse 1   Other female relative 5
Father 2   Came alone 6
Other male relative 3   On own but with children 7
Family 4   Combination of above (specify) 8
                                                                    Other (specify) 9

A6   In which area did you live when you first arrived in the UK?

Record area ....

A7   Who did you live with?

Family (nuclear) 1
Family (extended) 2
Lived alone 3
Lived on own but with children.............. 4
Other (specify) 5

A8   What do you recall of your first impressions about coming to this country? What can you remember
      about the first few weeks?
      (Probe: Was there anyone who helped you adjust to your new life?)

A9a Have you been back to Bangladesh since you arrived in the UK?
      Yes .... 1 (go to A9b)
      No .... 2 (go to Section B)

A9b If Yes
      How often have you been back to Bangladesh?

A9c Do you go to Bangladesh with other members of your family?
      Yes 1
      No 2

A9d How long do you usually stay in Bangladesh?

A9e What are your main reasons for going to Bangladesh?
(Probe: For any care responsibilities in Bangladesh? Any specific care tasks undertaken when in Bangladesh)

A9f Taking your last visit, what were the main changes which you noticed in Bangladesh?

Section B: Marriage

All

B1 Can I just check, are you? (read out)
Married .... 1 (go to B2)
Single .... 2 (go to C1)
Widowed .... 3 (go to B14)
Divorced .... 4 (go to B17)
Separated .... 5 (go to B17)

B2 **If married**
(Probe: If married before and code as appropriate below)

B2a Respondent married once only 1

B2b Respondent married more than once .... 2 (Probe)

B2c Spouse married once only 3

B2d Spouse married more than once .... 4 (Probe)

B3 In which year did you get married?
Write in year

B4 How old were you when you got married?
Enter years

B5 Where did you get married?

B6 (If married in Bangladesh): How long after your marriage did your husband return to the UK?

B7 How many visits did he make to see you before you came to the UK?

B8 Can you describe your marriage process a little? (first marriage if married more than once)
(Probe and record details and circle relevant number)

Parents/elders chose, consent was not asked 1
Parents/elders chose, consent was asked 2
Respondent chose but parents/elders had the final say 3
Respondent chose and informed parents 4
Respondent chose but did not inform her parents 5

(Probe feelings about marriage process)

B9 What do you remember about the first year or so that you were married?
(Probe: How do you feel that your life changed?)

B10 Did you have to care for any of your in-laws at this time?
Yes 1
No 2

B11a Thinking of your marriage now, do you find time to spend with your husband?
Yes .... 1 (go to B11b)
No .... 2 (go to B12)

B11b If Yes
What sort of things do you do together?

B12 Do you know your husband's age?
Estimate in years
(Check respondent's age at A1c)

Husband's age not known .... 99 (go to B13)

B13 Is your husband's age close to your own?
Roughly the same 1
(up to 5 years older/younger)
Husband slightly older 2
(up to 10 years)
Husband considerably/a great deal older 3
(above 11 years)
Husband younger 4
(6 years or more)

W/D/S/S B14 – B19 If married go to Section C

If widowed
B14 May I ask when you were widowed?

Write in year

B15 Did this happen when you were living in the UK?
Yes 1
No 2

B16 How has your life changed since your husband died?
(Probe: Financial issues, emotional support, loneliness)

Have you been back to Bangladesh since you were widowed?
Yes 1
No 2

If divorced/separated
B17 May I ask when you were divorced or separated?

Write in year

B18 Did this happen when you were living in the UK?
Yes 1
No 2

B19 How has your life changed since your divorce/separation?

Section C: Household structure and children

I would now like to gather a few facts about you and the other people in your household.

C1   Including yourself, other adults and any children, how many people are there in this household, that is people who normally live here and either share one meal a day with you OR share the use of the living room with you?

Enter number of people   ☐☐

Now complete the Household grid

(NB If there are more than six people in the household, enter information in order of people's ages [from oldest to youngest])

Household grid

Enter initials of each person in the household (starting with respondent)

C2 Relationship to respondent

	Respondent	Person 2	Person 3	Person 4	Person 5	Person 6
1) Respondent	1					
2) Spouse/partner		2	2	2	2	2
3) Brother/sister (including in-law, step and adoptive)		3	3	3	3	3
4) Parent (including in-law, step and adoptive)		4	4	4	4	4
5) Child (including step and adoptive)		5	5	5	5	5
6) Son-in-law/daughter-in-law		6	6	6	6	6
7) Grandchild (including step and adoptive)		7	7	7	7	7
8) Niece/nephew		8	8	8	8	8
9) Aunt/uncle		9	9	9	9	9
10) Other relative (including step and adoptive)		10	10	10	10	10
11) Other non-relative		11	11	11	11	11

C3 Sex

	Respondent	Person 2	Person 3	Person 4	Person 5	Person 6
1) Male		1	1	1	1	1
2) Female		2	2	2	2	2

Enter initials of each person in the household (starting with respondent)

C4 Relationship to respondent

	Person 7	Person 8	Person 9	Person 10	Person 11	Person 12
2) Spouse/partner	2	2	2	2	2	2
3) Brother/sister (including in-law, step and adoptive)	3	3	3	3	3	3
4) Parent (including in-law, step and adoptive)	4	4	4	4	4	4
5) Child (including step and adoptive)	5	5	5	5	5	5
6) Son-in-law/daughter-in-law	6	6	6	6	6	6
7) Grandchild (including step and adoptive)	7	7	7	7	7	7
8) Niece/nephew	8	8	8	8	8	8
9) Aunt/uncle	9	9	9	9	9	9
10) Other relative (including step and adoptive)	10	10	10	10	10	10
11) Other non-relative	11	11	11	11	11	11

C5 Sex

	Person 7	Person 8	Person 9	Person 10	Person 11	Person 12
1) Male	1	1	1	1	1	1
2) Female	2	2	2	2	2	2

C6 How many children do you have altogether?

Enter number of children   ☐☐

No children .... Code 99 (go to Section D)

C7 Have you lost any of your children?

(Probe: If child(ren) has died was this in Bangladesh or UK?)

C8 Could I just check the ages of your children and where they were born?

Child	Age	Sex	Where born
1			
2			
3			
4			
5			
6			
7			
8			
9			
10			

C9 Could I just check, whereabouts does your nearest child live?

1) No children in UK
2) Same house/same block
3) In Tower Hamlets
4) In another London borough (inner)
5) In another London borough (outer)
6) Elsewhere in the UK

C10a   Do any of your children live in Bangladesh?
        Yes..1 (go to C10b)
        No...2 (go to C11a)

C10b   If Yes
        How do you feel about this?
        (Probe: For when last seen and any concerns about the child(ren))

C11a   Could I ask if any of your children are married?
        Yes..1 (go to C11b)
        No...2 (go to Section D)

C11b Could I just confirm which ones are married?
        (Write in grid sex and age when married)
        (If single or no children go to Section D)

	Sex	Age when married	Where married	Country now resident
1				
2				
3				
4				
5				
6				
7				
8				
9				
10				

C12 How did you go about choosing your child's (or children's) partner(s)?
       (Open-ended, but tick one of the following)

       I chose my son/daughter-in-law, my son/daughter was not asked...1
       I chose my son/daughter-in-law, but the final decision was my son's/daughter's 2
       My son/daughter chose and then informed us 3
       My son/daughter chose and proceeded without my/our consent... 4

C13 What were the reasons for this method of choosing?

C14a Could I just check, have you any daughters who are not yet married?

Yes.. 1 (go to C14b)

No.....................................2 (go to Section D)

No daughters ....9 (go to Section D)

C14b How would you like them to get married?

C15 Would you like them to get married the same way as you did?

C16 What is your opinion of people choosing their own partners?

C17 How would you feel if your daughter chose her own partner?

Section D: Mother–daughter relations

We are interested in the way that mother–daughter relationships might have changed, could I ask you a few questions about this issue?

D1a Is your own mother living at present?

Yes.................... 1 (go to D1b)

No .... 2 (go to D2)

D1b If Yes

Where does your mother live?

Record area and country

To all

D2 What kind of relationship did you have with your mother when you were living in Bangladesh?

D3   What kind of relationship do you have now with your mother/or did have before she died?

D4a   (For those whose mothers are still alive)
      (Rest go to D5)

      How is your mother's health?
      Very good I
      Good 2
      Neither good nor poor 3
      Poor 4
      Very poor 5

D4b   If poor or very poor:
        Who takes care of your mother?

D4c   Are you able to offer any kind of support?
      (Probe: If so what kind of support can you offer?)

D5   Check C14a
        Ask only of those with daughter(s)
        (For those with no daughters go to Section E)

      How would you say your relationship with your daughter(s) compares with that to your own mother?

D6   Comparing your own life with that of your daughter(s), what do you see as the main differences (if any). Probe for positive/negative evaluation of these.

D7a   Are any of your daughter(s) in paid employment?
        Yes .... I (go to D7b)
        No .... 2 (go to D8)

D7b   What sort of jobs do they do?
        Record Daughter   I ....
                           2 ....
                           3 ....

D8   If No
      Would you like your daughter(s) to have paid employment?

D9 **To all**
Are there any jobs that you would not like your daughter(s) to do?

D10a Have any of your daughter(s) gone into further or higher education?
Yes .... 1 (go to D10b)
No .... 2 (go to Section E)

D10b If Yes
What courses are they doing?
(Probe: Respondent's views about these)

Section E: Relatives

E1 Apart from children, whereabouts does your nearest relative live?
(Do not include spouse)

No relatives in the UK 1
Same house/same block 2
In Tower Hamlets 3
In another London borough (inner) 4
In another London borough (outer) 5
Elsewhere in the UK 6

E2 Do you have any friends in this community/neighbourhood?
Yes .... 1 (go to E3)
No .... 2 (go to E5)

E3 How often do you have a chat or do something with one of your friends?
Never 1
Daily 2
2-3 times a week 3
At least weekly 4
At least monthly 5
Less often 6

E4 Are most of your friends from the Bangladeshi community?
Yes 1
No 2

E5 Do you have any friends from outside the community?
Yes 1
No 2

E5a If Yes

(Probe: Who and where do these friends come from?)

E6a Thinking back over the past five years, has there been a time when you needed help and support (for example, when you were ill)?

Yes .... 1 (go to E6b)

No .... 2 (go to E7a)

E6b If Yes

Was there someone available to help you?

Yes 1

No 2

E7a If you needed support in the future, would you have someone to whom you could turn?

Yes .... 1 (go to E7b)

No .... 2 (go to Section F)

E7b If Yes

Who would this person be?

Section F: Housing

F1 (Interviewer to code from observation)

What type of accommodation does the household live in?

Whole house/bungalow, detached 1

Whole house/bungalow, semi-detached 2

Whole house/bungalow, terraced/end of terrace 3

Purpose-built flat or maisonette in block with lift.. 4

Purpose-built flat or maisonette in block without lift 5

Converted flat or maisonette 6

Bedsit/rooms 7

Dwelling with business premises 8

Houseboat/caravan or mobile home 9

Flat in sheltered housing 10

Other (specify) 11

Could I ask a few questions about your housing and accommodation?

F2   How long have you lived in this house/flat?
Number of years   ☐☐

If less than one year enter number of months   ☐☐

F3   When you moved to this accommodation, from how far away did you move?
From within Tower Hamlets 1
From another London borough (inner) 2
From another London borough (outer) 3
Elsewhere in the UK 4
Abroad 5

F4   In whose name is the accommodation owned or rented?
Respondent only 1
Spouse/partner only 2
A family member only 3
Jointly – respondent and spouse/partner 4
Jointly – respondent and family member 5
Jointly – other combination 6
Someone else (not family) 7

F5   In which of these ways do you occupy this accommodation?
Own outright .... 1 (go to F7)
Buying it with the help of a mortgage or loan .... 2 (go to F7)
Pay part rent and part mortgage (shared ownership) .... 3 (go to F7)
Rent it .... 4 (ask F6)
Live here rent free (including rent-free in relative's/
friend's property: excluding squatting) .... 5 (go to F7)
Squatting .... 6 (go to F7)

F6   If rents only
Who do you rent this accommodation from?

Organisations
Local authority or council 1
New Town Corporation or Commission 2
Housing association/co-operative/charitable trust 3
Property company 4
Employer 5
Other organisation (specify and code) 6

Individuals
Relative 7
Employer 8
Other individual (including private landlord) 9

F7   Ask all
Excluding toilets, kitchens and bathrooms, how many rooms do you have in your accommodation?

Number of rooms   ☐☐

F8   How many of these rooms are used as bedrooms, including bed-sitting rooms and spare bedrooms?

Number of rooms   ☐☐

F9   Overall, how satisfied are you with this accommodation?
Very satisfied I
Fairly satisfied 2
Neither satisfied nor dissatisfied 3
Slightly dissatisfied 4
Very dissatisfied 5

F10   Do you have any of the following problems with your accommodation?
(Read out problems and code answer for each)

	Yes, has a problem	No, doesn't have a problem
Shortage of space	I	2
Too dark, not enough light	I	2
Lack of adequate heating facilities	I	2
Leaky roof	I	2
Damp walls, floors, foundations, etc	I	2
Rot in window frames or floors	I	2
Mould	I	2
No place to sit outside, eg, a terrace, patio or garden	I	2
Unsuitable for my physical disability(ies)/my state of health	I	2

F11   Do you have any other problems with your accommodation?
Yes I
No .... 2 (go to instruction above F12)

If yes
(Probe for details)

If any problems identified at F10 or F11, ask F12

F12   Has your health or the health of anyone in your household been made worse by your housing situation?
Yes I
No 2

Section G: Neighbourhood

I would like to ask some questions about the neighbourhood where you live and what it is like living here.

G1   What do you call the neighbourhood you live in?
       (If necessary, prompt: If you had to tell a friend where you lived, what would you tell them?)

G2   How long have you lived in this neighbourhood?

       Enter number of years .... ☐☐

       If less than one year, enter number of months .... ☐☐

G3   Where did you live immediately before moving to this neighbourhood?

       If respondent has always lived in neighbourhood, Code 96

G4a   Thinking about this neighbourhood, is there anything you particularly like about living here?
       Yes 1   (ask G4b)
       No 2   (go to G5a)

G4b   If Yes
       What? (Probe fully, record verbatim)

G5a   Is there anything you particularly dislike about living in this neighbourhood?
       Yes .... 1 (ask G5b)
       No .... 2 (go to G6)

G5b   If Yes
       What? (Probe fully)

G6   In general, how satisfied are you with this neighbourhood as a place to live?
       Very satisfied 1
       Fairly satisfied 2
       Neither satisfied nor dissatisfied 3
       Fairly dissatisfied 4
       Very dissatisfied 5

G7 I am now going to read out some things that you may or may not worry about. Please tell me how worried you are about each of them.
Read out statements and code answer for each

	Very worried	Fairly worried	Not very worried	Not at all worried
Having your home broken into and something stolen	I	2	3	4
Being mugged or robbed	I	2	3	4
Being physically attacked because of your colour	I	2	3	4
Being physically attacked because of your ethnic origin or religion	I	2	3	4

G8 How safe would you feel if you had to go out alone in this neighbourhood after dark?
(Read out all options and code only one)
Very safe I
Fairly safe 2
A bit unsafe 3
Very unsafe 4

G9 How safe do you feel when you are in your own home at night?
(Read out all options and code only one)
Very safe I
Fairly safe 2
A bit unsafe 3
Very unsafe 4

Section H: Family support

HI Check below and record
Children aged under 12 I
Children aged 12-15 2
Children aged 16 and above 3
No children 4

For those with no children under 12 go to H4

H2 First, could I check, are you involved in paid work outside the home?
Yes .... I (go to H3)
No .... 2 (go to H4)

H3   Where children are under 12

Can I just check who looks after your children aged under 12 while you are working?

Respondent works only while they are at school 1
They look after themselves until respondent gets home 2
Spouse looks after them 3
Mother/mother-in law looks after them 4
They go to a workplace nursery 5
Day nursery 6
A relative looks after them 7
An older child looks after them 8
A friend or neighbour looks after them 9
Other (specify) 10
Can't say 11

H4   (Apart from children under 12) is there anyone living with you or staying with you at the moment who you personally look after or give special help to? I am thinking of people who may need help because they are sick, or have disabilities or who are elderly?
Yes .... 1 (go to H5)
No .... 2 (go to Section I)

H5   If yes
Who is it that you look after?

(Write in forenames and person number(s) from the household grid)

Name	Person number
1	☐☐
2	☐☐
3	☐☐

H6   Could you describe the care you provide?

H7   Do you feel that you need more help (for example, from local services) in providing this care?

H8   Is there anyone else you are not living with who you give special help to?
Yes .... 1 (go to H9)
No .... 2 (go to Section I)

H9   Could you describe the care you provide?

Section I: Experiences of everyday life

I1   Could you describe for me a typical day in your life, starting from the morning and going through to the evening?

I2   Thinking about the sort of day you have described, how does this compare with one which you might have if you were living in ... [name area from which they came] in Bangladesh?

I3a   Do you have any worries in your life at the present time?
      (If no go to Section J)

I3b   If Yes
      What would you say are your main worries?

I3c   How do you see these as being resolved?
      (Probe whether external support from local services of any description might be helpful)

Section J: Health and well-being

I would now like to ask some questions about your health

J1a   Would you say that for someone of your age, your own health is generally:
      (Read out)
      1)   Very good
      2)   Good
      3)   Neither good nor poor
      4)   Poor
      5)   Very poor

JIb   Do you have any long-standing illness, disability or infirmity? By long-standing, I mean anything that has troubled you over a period of time or that is likely to affect you over a period of time?
Yes .... I (go to JIc)
No .... 2 (go to J2)

JIc   What is this condition?
(Probe fully. Record verbatim)

JId   Does this illness or disability (Do any of these illnesses or disabilities) limit your activities in any way?
Yes .... I (go to JIe)
No .... 2 (go to J2)

JIe   In what way(s)?
(Probe fully. Record verbatim)

J2   Could I just check are you registered with a GP?
Yes I
No 2

J3a   Over the past month, approximately how many times have you talked to, or visited a GP or family doctor about your own health? Please do not include any visits to a hospital, or any visits you made while abroad.
I)   One or two times   (go to J3b)
2)   Three to five times   (go to J3b)
3)   Six to ten times   (go to J3b)
4)   More than ten times   (go to J3b)
5)   None   (go to J4)

If visited in past month

J3b   Is your doctor Bengali?
Yes .... I (go to J4)
No .... 2 (go to J3c)

J3c   If No
How do you communicate with him or her?

J4   Do you have or have you ever had any of the following conditions?
      (Read out and ring one code for each)

	Yes	No
High blood pressure, sometimes called hypertension (apart from during pregnancy)	I	2
A stroke	I	2
Diabetes	I	2
Angina	I	2
A heart attack – including a heart murmur	I	2
A damaged heart or rapid heart	I	2

J5   How would you describe your mental state?
      (Probe: If you feel bad, what do you do?)

J6   Could I ask you some questions about your general health?
      Have you recently:

J6.1 Been able to concentrate on what you are doing?

Better than usual ☐   Less than usual ☐

Same as usual ☐   Much less than usual ☐

J6.2 Lost much sleep over worry?

Not at all ☐   Rather more than usual ☐

No more than usual ☐   Much more than usual ☐

J6.3 Felt that you are playing a useful part in things?

More so than usual ☐   Less useful than usual ☐

Same as usual ☐   Much less capable ☐

J6.4 Felt capable of making decisions about things?

More so than usual ☐   Less so than usual ☐

Same as usual ☐   Much less capable ☐

J6.5 Felt constantly under strain?

Not at all ☐   Rather more than usual ☐

No more than usual ☐   Much more than usual ☐

J6.6 Felt you could not overcome your difficulties?

Not at all ☐   Rather more than usual ☐

No more than usual ☐   Much more than usual ☐

J6.7 Been able to enjoy your normal day-to-day activities?

More so than usual ☐   Less than usual ☐

Same as usual ☐   Much less than usual ☐

J6.8 Been able to face up to your problems?

More so than usual ☐   Less able than usual ☐

Same as usual ☐   Much less able ☐

J6.9 Been feeling unhappy and depressed?

Not at all ☐   Rather more than usual ☐

No more than usual ☐   Much more than usual ☐

J6.10 Been losing confidence in yourself?

Not at all ☐   Rather more than usual ☐

No more than usual ☐   Much more than usual ☐

J6.11 Been thinking of yourself as a worthless person?

Not at all ☐   Rather more than usual ☐

No more than usual ☐   Much more than usual ☐

J6.12 Been feeling reasonably happy, all things considered?

More so than usual ☐   Less so than usual ☐

About the same as usual ☐   Much less than usual ☐

Section K: Religion and identity

K1   In terms of religion and identity, how would you describe yourself?
(Ring those mentioned)

Bengali 1
Muslim 2
Sylheti 3
British 4
Other 5

K2   Which of those you have mentioned (if more than one) is most important to you?

K3   How important is your faith to your life?

Section L: Work status

Could I just ask you some questions about work outside the home?

L1   Could I just check, are you doing paid work of any kind outside the home?
(Record code which best fits the respondent)

(Code one only)

Looking after the family, home or dependants .... 1 (got to L3)
In paid work, including self-employment .... 2 (got to L2)
Unemployed/not working .... 3 (got to L3)
Wholly retired from paid work .... 4 (got to L3)
Unable to work because of long-term disability or health .... 5 (got to L3)
In full-time education or training (including government training programme) .... 6 (got to L3)
Doing something else (specify) .... 7 (got to L3)

L2   If in paid work

Explore the kind of work and check on the following:
In full-time paid work, including self-employment (31 or more hours per week) .... 1 (got to L5)
In part-time paid work, including self-employment (8-30 hours per week) .... 1 (got to L5)
In part-time paid work, including self-employment (less than 8 hours per week) .... 1 (got to L5)

L3   If not in paid work last week

Have you ever been in paid employment or been self-employed?
Yes .... 1 (go to L5)
No .... 2 (go to L4)

L4   If not or never in paid work
Would you like to have paid work outside the home?
(Probe whether would like training and obstacles to paid work)

L5   If ever in paid work
How old were you when you were last in paid work?
Write in age in years

L6   If currently/ever in paid work
Now I'd like to ask you about your current (most recent) job. What is (was) the name or title of your current (most recent) job?
(If two+ jobs at once, take the main job [if queried, most remunerative])

L7   What skills or qualifications are (were) needed for the job (if appropriate)?

L8   Interviewer check. Is respondent married or living as part of a couple?
      Yes .... I (go to L9)
      No .... 2 (go to Section M)

L9   If married/living as a couple
      .... Can I just check, is your husband/wife/partner in paid work?
      Yes .... I (go to L11)
      No .... 2 (go to L10)

L10   If No
      Has he/she ever been in paid work?
      Yes .... I (go to L11)
      No .... 2 (go to Section M)

L11   If spouse/partner was in paid work
      How long ago was he in paid work?
      Write in age in years
      (Estimate acceptable)

L12   If spouse/partner ever in paid work
      What is (was) the name or title of his/her current (most recent) job?
      (If two+ jobs at once, take main job [if queried, most remunerative])

L13   What skills or qualifications are (were) needed for the job?

Section M: Education, language and literacy

M1   At what age did you finish your continuous full-time education at school or college?

      Record age

      Or code: (no formal schooling)   97

M2   How far, or to what level, did you study?

M3a Have you been on any courses in this country?
Yes .... 1 (go to M3b)
No .... 2 (go to M4)

M3b If Yes
Please list the courses you have attended

M4 Could you list any educational qualifications, if any, which you have?

M5 Can you read and write Bengali?
Yes 1
No 2

M6 Can you read and write English?
Yes 1
No 2

M7 Interviewer code
Interview wholly in English 1
Interview partly in English, partly in Sylheti 2
Interview wholly in Sylheti 3

Section N: Finances

Could I just ask you a few questions about finances?

N1 How would you say you and your family are managing financially these days?
(Open-ended, probe for any difficulties)

N2a Do you ever have any spare cash to spend on yourself?
Yes .... 1 (go to N3a)
No .... 2 (go to N2b)

N2b If No
How do you feel about that?

N3a Who usually does the household shopping?

Respondent .... 1 (go to N3b)

Husband .... 2 (go to N4)

Other(s) (specify) .... 3 (go to N4)

N3b If respondent

Who usually pays for the household shopping?

Respondent 1

Husband 2

Other(s) (specify) 3

N4 Do you have access to any money in an emergency?

Yes 1

No 2

N5 In your household, who has the final say in big financial decisions?

Respondent 1

Spouse/partner 2

Both have equal say 3

Other (specify) 4

Cannot say 5

N6 Could you tell me about any benefits you are receiving?

(Code all that apply)

National Insurance Retirement (Old Age) Pension 1

Income Support 2

Housing Benefit, rent rebate or rent allowance 3

Council Tax Benefit or rebate 4

Working Families' Tax Credit (Family Credit) 5

Child Benefit (including One Parent Benefit) 6

Jobseeker's Allowance (Unemployment Benefit) 7

Widow's or War Widow's Pension 8

Other widow's benefit (eg, Widowed Mother's Allowance) 9

Bereavement Benefit 10

Disability Living Allowance/Mobility Allowance/Attendance Allowance 11

Severe Disablement Allowance/Industrial Disablement Benefit/Incapacity Benefit 12

Invalid Care Allowance 13

Other state benefit(s) (specify) 14

N7 Do you get any regular payments of any kind?

(Code all that apply)

Earnings from employment or self-employment   1

Pension from a previous employer (occupational pension)   2

Pension from a spouse's previous employer (occupational pension)	3
Private pension/annuity	4
Income and dividends from shares and investments	5
Other kinds of regular allowance from outside the household	6
Income from other sources, eg, rent, savings	7
None of these	8

N8 Could you give me a rough estimate of your weekly household income?
Include income from all sources including benefits, interest on savings, rental income, maintenance, etc.
Take estimate if necessary. Enter band:

£ ☐ ☐ ☐ ☐

N9a Do any of your children make a financial contribution to the running of your home?
Yes .... 1 (go to N9b)
No .... 2 (go to Section O)

N9b If Yes
Is this done on a regular basis (say every week or month)?
Yes 1
No 2

Section O: The future

Finally, could I just finish the interview with some questions about the future?

O1   How much has your life changed since you came to the UK from Bangladesh?

O2   What are your hopes for the future?

O3   Where do you see yourself in, say, five years time?

Thinking about some of the issues we have talked about, is there anything that you yourself would like to raise or tell me about?

Many thanks for your time and for your help with this study.

Section P: Interviewer observations

P1   Were any other people present during the interview?
    1)   Yes
    2)   No

If Yes
Write identity(ies) of other person(s) present (eg, husband, daughter, neighbour, etc)

P2   Did any of these people seem to influence any of the answers given by the respondent?
    1)   A great deal
    2)   A fair amount
    3)   A little
    4)   Not at all

In what way was the respondent influenced?
(Note particular questions)

P3   In general, the respondent's cooperation during the interview was:
    1)   Very good
    2)   Good
    3)   Fair
    4)   Poor
    5)   Very poor

Time interview finished:

Appendix C: Researching minority ethnic communities: reflections on working in the field

An important issue raised by this research and similar projects concerns how best to approach minority ethnic groups such as those represented in South Asian communities. Particular problems may relate, for example, to ensuring random samples of respondents, securing interviews, recruiting skilled researchers and interviewers in the case of non-English speaking groups, and making contact with diverse community organisations. This Appendix represents both some reflections on these issues arising from the research discussed in this report, as well as drawing on comments from experts in the field, including academics, health and social care professionals, and representatives from community groups representing ethnic minorities[1]. These reflections focus on issues related to community-based research rather than national surveys and explore six main areas:

- accessing communities
- accessing individuals
- developing research instruments
- entering the field
- exiting the field
- future research

Accessing communities

Community-based research raises particular issues as regards the dual need to gain credibility among key

stakeholders and (depending on the nature of the study) individual respondents. The key steps in this process will almost certainly be:

- First, being as clear as possible about the research objectives, and ensuring that the 'story about the research' is maintained consistently across different organisations and individuals.
- Second, recognising and (hopefully) building on the work of previous researchers working in the locality.
- Third, tailoring the explanation about the research in a way that meets the needs of different audiences.

Typical methods in respect of the last of these might include:

- leaflets aimed at community organisations;
- seminars to professional audiences;
- informal presentations to community groups.

The research presented in this report utilised all of these formats. At an early stage of the study, leaflets (in English and Sylheti) were distributed to health centres in the borough, around housing estates and through organisations representing women. It is difficult to gauge the impact of publicity of this kind, but leaflets do help to raise the profile of the work to be undertaken, and can prove valuable when visiting organisations and seeing potential respondents. An outline of the research was presented, soon after securing the grant, to the Tower Hamlets Community Research Network (see following), which led to some important contacts in the area.

---

[1] A range of individuals were consulted in organisations in Tower Hamlets and other London boroughs.

Finally, soon after her appointment, the research fellow employed on the project visited a number of community groups to give short presentations about the aims and objectives of the study.

Researchers from outside the community face the issue of explaining their objectives to established groups who may have strong views about the way in which research should be conducted. Organising an advisory group that meets on a regular basis can be especially helpful in this regard, for example in drawing attention to networks and resources that might assist the research. Again, it may also be the case (as happened in this study) that particular individuals are able to offer informal advice and assistance through the duration of the project.

Gaining the support of community groups will certainly be helpful in increasing awareness about key issues that need to be resolved. However, another dimension is that where successful, such assistance can help in reducing the isolation experienced by lone community researchers – an acute problem in the fieldwork phase of research. In this regard, project management needs to consider the most appropriate support network to assist workers in the field. For some localities, there may be a number of research projects already underway and some mutual support is worth considering. In this study, the Community Research Network existing in the borough was a valuable forum as a sounding board for ideas and learning about the existence of other research projects in the locality.

Accessing individuals

The initial work will also be vital for drawing a sample of respondents. In this research, a wide range of options was considered for accessing a group who may be hard to contact in community settings. The answer to questions of access will depend to some degree on the group being studied. In this case, a sample of women (most of whom were likely to have children) suggested that working with health centres and drawing on age/sex registers was always likely to be the best option. The majority of women of reproductive age in an area are likely to be registered with a general practitioners, in contrast with their involvement with other organisations where under-representation is likely to be a much greater problem.

Moreover, some sampling options (for example snowballing or 'cold calling' around particular residential clusters) may produce restricted samples in the sense that only a limited range of social networks may be drawn upon. Working solely through community organisations may also produce complications. Castles et al, for example, identify the need to move away from community-based contacts in selecting interviews, and to seek '... *alternative ways to access immigrant and refugee populations in order to include marginalised individuals*' (2001, p 10; our emphasis). They go on to warn that in relation to community organisations: "The people interviewed are often those who are already active in [migrant] communities or people who have already accessed services successfully, hence their 'voices' may not be representative" (Castles, 2001, p 102).

Developing research instruments

Despite their limitations in relation to accessing a sample, community organisations have an important role in assisting in the development of the research instrument (in the case of this research the questionnaire used in the interview). At the beginning of the study, the research team had a list of topics that had been identified in the original application to the Nuffield Foundation. However, there were many issues to be considered in moving to a structured questionnaire that would work in the field. Here, going through both pre-pilot and pilot stages of research was essential. The pre-pilot phase, conducted through individuals recruited through community organisations, was valuable in providing an initial feel for the range of issues affecting the target group of respondents. Some questions the researchers knew had to be asked, for example about the nature of the household, caring responsibilities, and relationships within the neighbourhood. Others, such as the characteristics of transnational ties and the experience of migration, were less clear and required a considerable amount of development. Following the pilot phase, the draft questionnaire was then circulated around the advisory group and some community organisations, producing various amendments and a final redrafting. Again, having comments from people actively involved with (in our case) Bangladeshi women, was of enormous assistance in improving the quality of the final product.

Entering the field

At one level, researching minority ethnic groups (whether South Asian or any other) is no different to most forms of social research, involving as it does issues of confidentiality, respect for the individual respondent, and sensitivity when approaching particular topics. On the other hand, there may be particular characteristics of the group being researched that does have implications for the organisation and conduct of the work. Clearly, researchers need to be observant of cultural and religious events, such as Eid, Ramadan and Diwali; periods when respondents may be unavailable or have increased responsibilities. In this study, periods of fasting or particular times for prayer were important issues to be considered when arranging interviews.

More general cultural practices and standards of behaviour also need to be acknowledged: wearing clothing that will not give offence, taking shoes off when entering a home, accepting tea when offered. And the conduct of the interview itself may raise issues that go beyond the usual rules for such encounters. For example, body language and eye contact show marked cross-cultural variation (abstaining from direct eye contact is a sign of respect amongst South Asian communities rather than a lack of confidence).

Some of these points confirm the value of ethnic and gender matching when undertaking research. Some of the benefits of the former identified by academics and practitioners in the field include:

- The respondent is more likely to feel relaxed and open and less likely to be intimidated than if interviewed by a white person.
- Ethnically matched researchers are likely to take a more emphatic approach.
- Ethnic matching can help build immediate rapport and trust.
- Ethnic matching means that people do not have to explain aspects of their culture, religion or way of thinking.

The gender of the researcher is also likely to be relevant when working with South Asian communities. A woman whose interactions are limited to family, close friends and neighbours may feel wary about talking to a male stranger, especially if such behaviour is regarded as culturally aberrant. Language is also crucial and the importance of recruiting a researcher able to speak the main language of the group under study is vital. Depending on the scale of the research, relying on teams of interpreters can bring problems. Recruitment and retention can be difficult and the reliability of data can be compromised. Moreover, building research skills within minority ethnic groups needs to be considered, and in this context over-reliance on interpreters must be regarded as meeting short-term rather than long-term needs.

Exiting the field

Leaving the field presents particular issues and concerns in relation to minority ethnic communities. Clearly, if much of the preparatory work has been devoted to assuring stakeholders of the potential value of the research, then detailed attention to dissemination is equally important. From our consultation with community practitioners, there remains the feeling that feedback is a neglected aspect of the research process. Essentially, though, it needs to be seen as the mirror image of the initial phase of entering the field with researchers exploiting the full range of options including:

- summaries of the main report (translated in the language of the community in question);
- briefing papers;
- presentations to community groups;
- academic papers;
- conferences.

The difficulty here is whether this additional layer of dissemination is fully costed in the research proposal, and whether communities feel themselves to be involved in the dissemination.

Future research

These reflections suggest that within minority ethnic communities working needs to be built around some key areas of good practice, especially in relation to accessing communities, accessing individuals, developing research instruments, entering the field and exiting the field. Migrant populations present specific challenges for social research, especially in respect of gaining access to representative samples and recruiting staff with language and related skills appropriate to the group in question. Further work is justified by the main grant-giving bodies, and professional bodies such as the British Sociological Association, in ensuring that research skills and research capacity can meet the changing nature of the migrant population in the UK.

Some of the issues that require additional research are identified by Castles et al (2001) in their report *Integration: Mapping the field*. They highlight a number of points relevant to the issues raised in this particular study. These include:

- The need for longitudinal research exploring the integration and adaptation of migrant communities.
- The importance of comparative research. In the case of this study, further investigation as to the differences between the Tower Hamlets population and other Bangladeshi communities is urgently needed.
- More work is needed on transnational ties and the way in which these change over time.
- Social action research is required which involves migrant groups in the design of their own research.
- Further work is needed on how language and culture is maintained through first and later generations.
- The specific issues facing women and older migrants needs further research, especially as these groups may be vulnerable to various forms of abuse and dependency within their social networks.
- The broad issue of the position of immigrant women in the family and community needs to be addressed.

These and other questions set out an important agenda for future research. An important start has been made, by various researchers, in the case of the Bangladeshi community, especially in the context of Tower Hamlets. However, it will be important to build on the concerns this body of research, and other work with minority ethnic groups, has raised to secure a clearer grasp of the issues that migrant communities are likely to face in the future.